INHERITANCE AND WEALTH INEQUALITY IN BRITAIN

Inheritance and Wealth Inequality in Britain

C. D. HARBURY and
D. M. W. N. HITCHENS
The City University, London

London
GEORGE ALLEN & UNWIN
Boston   Sydney

First published in 1979

GEORGE ALLEN & UNWIN LTD
40 Museum Street, London WC1A 1LU

© C. D. Harbury and D. M. W. N. Hitchens, 1979

British Library Cataloguing in Publication Data

Harbury, Colin Desmond
  Inheritance and wealth inequality in Britain.
  1. Wealth – Great Britain
  2. Inheritance and succession – Great Britain
  I. Title   II. Hitchens, D. M. W. N.
  339.4'1'0941   HC260.W4   79-40476

ISBN 0-04-330296-3

Typeset in 10 on 11 point Times by Servis Filmsetting Ltd, Manchester
and printed in Great Britain by Unwin Brothers Ltd, Old Woking, Surrey

Preface

This book tries to assess the role of inheritance in the distribution of personal wealth in Britain during the present century. It is heavily empirical and the authors would hope its main contribution is seen as providing quantitative evidence of a direct kind on this important matter, including the sources of the fortunes of a number of large wealth leavers in the 1950s, 1960s and 1970s.

The initial work on which the book is based was undertaken with help from two grants of financial assistance from the Houblon-Norman Fund to C. D. Harbury. The main research, however, was made possible by a grant from the Social Science Research Council. Grateful thanks are due to both of these organisations and also to The City University, the University of Birmingham and Trent University, Ontario, Canada, all of whom gave help and encouragement of various kinds.

So many people have knowingly and unknowingly offered help and advice over the many years during which this book has been in preparation that it is impossible to name them all. We must, however, unquestionably single out as the main recipient of our gratitude Professor S. J. Prais. His influence is to be found throughout the book but the basic structure of Chapter 7 (and Appendices D and E) is in particular due to his advice. Others whose help we particularly wish to acknowledge are A. B. Atkinson, A. J. Harrison, P. C. McMahon and N. Bosanquet. We should also like to thank a number of officials of the Department of Inland Revenue (especially Messrs Astin, Bugden, Butler, Dunn, Ganguly and King), the Principal Probate Registry, the General Registry Office, the Estate Duty Office, and Smee and Ford, the London Press Agency, whose help in connection with data sources was particularly valuable. The number of persons who assisted in the collection of data over the years goes well into double figures. We acknowledge with gratitude the help from J. Gilbert, S. Gooders, C. Hill, D. Howell, E. Kyle, E. Lawrence, D. Loveridge, G. S. Nagra, J. Prange, P. Scott, W. Shields and A. Snook. Mary Keane and Kath Vickers most patiently typed and retyped the manuscript. To all the above mentioned and unmentioned we express our thanks. We of course are responsible for any errors and omissions that remain.

C. D. HARBURY

D. M. W. N. HITCHENS

The City University, London

Contents

The Relationship between Fathers' Wealth and Wealth of Fathers-in-law
Mothers' Wealth
The Independent Wealth of Mothers
Wealth Transmission over Three Generations
Three Generations of Wealth Holders
Family Wealth Trees

Trends in Women's Wealth Shares
The Wealth of Fathers
The Wealth of Husbands
The Wealth of Fathers and Husbands
'Self-Made' Women
The Wealth of Fathers-in-law
Husbands' and Fathers' Wealth
Intermarriage Among the Rich
Mothers' Wealth
Conclusions

Location
Status
Occupation
Age

Galton's Technique
Method
The Contribution of Inheritance 1902–34
The Results for Other Periods
Confidence Limits
Explanations
Qualifications and Conclusions

The Nature and Reliability of the Data
Patterns of Inheritance
The Importance of Predecessors' Wealth
The Wealth of Fathers and Sons (Backward Tracing Samples)
Inheritors versus Self-Made Among Top Wealth Leavers
Trends in the Father-Son Wealth Relationship among Top and
    Medium Wealth Leavers

1

Introduction:
The Importance of Inheritance

> This small inheritance my father left me
> Contenteth me, and worth a monarchy.
> I seek not to wax great by others waning;
> Or gather wealth, I care not with what envy:
> Sufficeth that I have maintains my state,
> And sends the poor well pleased from my gate.
>   William Shakespeare, *King Henry VI, Part II*

Men of wealth and power are often the subject of admiration, envy and suspicion. Society does not quite know whether to regard them as heroes or as villains. This is partly because of uncertainty about the extent to which economic progress depends upon the drive for the acquisition of personal wealth by individuals. It is also because of doubt about the means whereby wealth is acquired – i.e. whether through inheritance or as a result of a man's own activities.

THE IMPORTANCE OF INHERITANCE

Economists have become interested in matters of distribution as well as of resource allocation in recent years as a result of the failure of traditional economics to provide policy guidance about efficiency independent of distribution. Their interest reflects also the values of a society where distributive shares are a matter of *mass* concern, whether because of the prominence they receive in discussions of incomes policies, because of the realisation that certain goods and services are inherently limited in supply and cannot be shared out (Hirsch, 1977), or because of new views of philosophers and political scientists on the nature of distributive justice (Rawls, 1972). The appointment of a standing Royal Commission on the Distribution of Income and Wealth (henceforth referred to as the Diamond Commission) is another obvious sign of general concern with this subject.

A subsidiary feature of the interest in distribution in present-day Britain is that it relates not only to income but also to wealth. Indeed, research into wealth shares has recently enjoyed a vogue greater than at any time since the 1920s. There seem to be two main reasons for this. The first is that it is much more unequally distributed than is income. The second is that the structure of taxation in Britain until relatively recently discriminated heavily against income and in favour of wealth, wealth acquisitions and capital gains. This benefited those people who could switch back and forth between income, wealth and capital gains to reduce their tax liabilities and penalised others, largely wage earners, who could not.

The appearance first of the capital gains tax in 1962, and then of the capital transfer tax (CTT) in 1974 (and even of the promise of a wealth tax) are all indicative of the view that the basis for taxation should be extended to wealth.[1] There is, moreover, a further feature of the interest in wealth distribution that is underlined by CTT – the first major and direct tax on gifts this country has known. This is that it recognised that wealth acquired by inheritance and other gifts should be the subject of special taxation and treated differently from wealth acquired in other ways. This reflects a view, widely held, that society *benefits* from the efforts of self-made men in the accumulation of capital, and that this should therefore be encouraged.[2] Indeed the very words 'inherited' and 'earned' carry with them the overtones of society's current moral values. To recognise the strength of this feeling is not, of course, to admit that all inherited wealth is reprehensible while all the activities of self-made men are meritorious. It is obvious that some fortunes have been amassed at great cost to society. At the same time one can allow that some highly enjoyable attributes of our culture might well not exist were it not for the presence of, for example, patrons of the arts with inherited wealth.

We are not concerned here to argue the various sides of the moral issue.[3] It is sufficient to observe the strength of feeling that inherited wealth should be differentially heavily taxed. Such a view is not a new one. Over fifty years ago Rignano (1926) was able to persuade some of the members of the Committee on National Debt and Taxation (Cmd 2800) that the principle underlying his scheme for encouraging saving and thrift by raising the rate of death duties every time wealth passed from one generation to the next was attractive. Rignano's proposals were regarded as impracticable at the time. Today they would be even more difficult to operate since the rapid changes in the price level would make it virtually impossible to identify most inheritances as they passed down the line from generation to generation. A specific piece of property is not always even reliably identified at the first passage. Yet if one wishes to tax inherited wealth differently from that which is 'earned', it is essential to be able to quantify the portion of wealth that is inherited.

QUANTIFYING INHERITANCE

There are three broad ways in which one can try to estimate the importance of inheritance in the distribution of personal wealth – as a residual, by the use of proxies and directly.

The residual approach makes use of the life cycle hypothesis discussed by Atkinson and others (Atkinson, 1971; Diamond, 1975, 1977). If one can account for the extent to which the distribution of personal wealth at any particular time can be explained by saving and the age (and sex) distribution of the population, then the remainder can be attributed, *inter alia*, to inheritance. Unfortunately the quantification of inheritance using this method is greatly hindered by data deficiencies and is very sensitive to differing assumptions, particularly about earnings and savings profiles in the period over which the life cycle model extends.

Recently the Diamond Commission (1977) have attempted to quantify the proportion of inherited to total personal wealth by aggregating the flow of total inheritances over a number of years by means of the perpetual inventory method in order to arrive at the stock of inherited wealth.

Another approach is to tackle the issue more directly by estimating the relationship between wealth of different generations of the same family. Given the problems of obtaining reliable data on personal wealth holdings, there is a case for using proxies for wealth in the process, so long as there is reason to believe that they are associated with size of wealth holdings. A very recent important contribution using this approach for the USA is by Brittain (1977) whose study relies heavily on such details as the income, occupation, education and residential characteristics of different members of the same family. The advantages of the method are largely in the availability of data. The disadvantages relate to the extent to which proxy measures are associated with wealth. The inadequacy of wealth data itself makes it hard to know whether the correlations would be high. The need to distinguish and quantify separately the association between wealth of fathers and sons and between their incomes is one important reason why direct evidence on wealth is of value.[4] That is why the approach adopted in this book employs estimates of personal wealth.

THE FORTUNES OF FATHERS, SONS AND OTHER RELATIVES

The chapters which follow are largely devoted to comparisons of the wealth at death of fathers and sons during the period 1902–73. In addition, certain data are presented on wealth association between members of the same family other than fathers and sons including grandfathers, husbands, fathers-in-law, mothers, daughters etc.

It is important to emphasise that our concern is almost exclusively with estimating the inherited component in the distribution of personal wealth and not with other non-pecuniary inherited characteristics. To the extent that parents pass on to their children advantages of education, genetic talents, social contacts, etc., money wealth is clearly a limited measure of what may be inherited, though the limits should not be exaggerated. Many of the excluded advantages that a privileged child inherits may lead him to accumulate above average wealth himself through, for example, the possession of 'superior' education or genes or through social contacts made at school which lead to business opportunities in later life, or even to a wealthy spouse.

THE NATURE OF WEALTH

It will become clear in Chapter 2 that the estimates of wealth that are used in this study are, perforce, based on a concept that is neither as complete nor as comprehensive as would be ideal. It is useful, however, to consider whether it is possible to set up a notional standard of wealth against which others can be judged. It can be argued that there is no single unambiguous definition of wealth of universal application. Rather are there several alternative wealth concepts, each of which is more or less suited to a particular purpose or policy issue. Take, for example, the macro-economic policy objectives of growth, price stability and full employment. These are liable to be influenced by the distribution of wealth. The effectiveness of investment may be illustrated by capital output ratios, for the estimation of which real rather than financial assets are then mainly relevant. There is likely to be more interest too in assets such as plant and equipment than in the stock of dwellings. Nevertheless, financial assets are also relevant to such matters as savings propensities when the effectiveness of counter-inflationary policies are under discussion.

More relevant than the stock of real and tangible assets to matters of inheritance is the total of personal wealth and its size distribution. For such distributive issues the appropriate wealth concept is at once broader though it may also, in another sense, be narrower. It is broader in that a person's wealth should embrace all real or financial assets, the possession of which provide purchasing power over goods and services, and include therefore even paper claims like the national debt, which do not of themselves give a title to a real asset. At the same time the relevant concept may be narrower if it is thought proper to exclude corporate, publicly owned and other assets. To take an example for purposes of illustration, if one is mainly interested in the distribution of economic power among wealth holders, one might consider excluding all assets other than voting shares in the major corporations in the country.

ESTIMATION PROBLEMS

Recognition that real and financial assets which give purchasing power should be included in personal wealth does not eliminate difficult problems. These are broadly of three kinds:

(1) those related to the distinction between wealth and income;
(2) those associated with the inclusion or exclusion of so-called non-marketable assets;
(3) valuation problems.

Wealth and Income
Economists, not to mention incidentally tax lawyers, have traditionally differentiated wealth from income by reference to the fact that the former is a stock and the latter a flow. The distinction is designed to draw

an appropriate dividing line between them and causes difficulties only when one tries to measure either. A parallel distinction is that between consumption expenditure and capital expenditure in the national accounts. In principle all consumer durable goods should be counted as wealth until they are consumed. But as virtually all goods (as distinct from services) are to an extent durable and have positive lives, it is necessary to adopt conventions to provide reasonable working rules. In the National Accounts, for example, houses happen to be counted as investment goods, and television sets as consumption. The problem is not of great practical significance in this study, because the coverage of household goods in personal wealth is fairly comprehensive. But the issues should not be ignored mainly because the value of chattels is thought at times to be considerably understated in the inventories of assets on death – a major source of data. For individuals with relatively low wealth this can lead to a proportionately serious undervaluation of their assets.

Non-Marketed Assets
The types of problem discussed so far relate to the treatment of assets which are bought and sold, i.e. for which there is a market. A more serious issue, however, is the extent to which non-marketed assets should figure in an individual's wealth. Such assets include the human capital embodied in an educated person, personal pension rights, and even the psychic assets incorporated in a nation's 'cultural heritage'. There are two main reasons why assets may not be marketed. They may be non-transferable, or they may consist of rights to certain publicly provided goods or services.

Non-transferability may, for instance, be related to person-specific assets, such as annuities and pension rights, which cannot be sold. Although it is possible to imagine a market-place for such assets, difficulties would arise from the distinctively individual risk element attaching to each of them. Another explanation of non-transferability is that the current social mores may deem the sale of certain assets to be reprehensible, not to say illegal, though this may not, in itself, prevent their reaping a reward for their owners – as with prostitution.

A rather different type of asset which is person-specific and inherently non-transferable is the capital value of education. Its quantification is so fraught with difficulties that one is tempted to exclude it from the estimates of the net worth of an individual. The implications of such a decision may, however, be important. For example, if one is considering whether to impose a wealth tax, the decision to exclude human capital is likely to result in a heavier burden being placed on higher age groups (Sandford *et al.*, 1975; Neild, 1976). Education is, of course, supplied both in the private and public sectors. The latter provision raises also the wider issue of access to public goods and services such as state subsidised council housing. It is not generally thought desirable to allow those who qualify for this kind of low price service on grounds of residence, family circumstances etc. to sell their rights to others. Yet, if such rights are not included in personal wealth holdings of individuals, curious conclusions can be drawn from the statistics. For example, an administrative decision by local authorities to sell their council houses to occupants can apparently cause a reduction in the observed inequality of wealth.[5]

Valuation of Assets

Most valuation problems are well known and discussed at length in the literature (e.g. Revell, 1967). The starting point is usually that the best valuation for an asset is its market price. However, many business assets are more or less unique and have to be valued at cost, adjusted according to alternative accounting and other conventions for depreciation, and at replacement cost when prices are changing. Assets also often exhibit substantial differences between sale and purchase price – e.g. in the personal sector, household goods. The difference approximates to that between replacement cost and second-hand sale value.

In the business sector there are two main bases for asset valuation. Assets may be valued on a 'going concern' basis reflecting roughly the discounted value of the stream of future receipts or at the price they would sell for – their 'break-up' value. The appropriate basis depends naturally on the purpose of the exercise. For a man who inherits a family business, which he immediately sells in order to spend the proceeds on consumption, the realised price should apply, whereas if he kept the firm going, say, to leave it in his turn to his children, the 'going concern' value is the right one.

There are many other kinds of problems associated with the proper way to value assets, such as those in the public sector where there exists no market price, and those in monopolistic sectors where market price may be held artificially high. One difficulty which should perhaps be mentioned relates to the value of life assurance policies. These assets change value very substantially on the death of the person whose life is covered. Before that event the surrender value is usually only a fraction of that after death. This fact causes difficulties with regard to estimates of the wealth of individuals in this study and it is referred to again in the next chapter.

Finally, reference must be made to the major problems involved in constructing series relating to the distribution of wealth over an extended period of time. These arise largely from changes in the general level of prices for which some allowance must be made. The present study covers more than a hundred years and it was thought necessary to construct special index numbers to try to deal with these problems. They are derived and discussed in the next chapter.

THE SIZE DISTRIBUTION OF PERSONAL WEALTH IN BRITAIN

It is not the purpose of this book to describe in any detail the present state of the distribution of personal wealth in Britain or of past trends. This task has been undertaken recently by the Diamond Commission (1975, 1976, 1977) and by Atkinson and Harrison (1978). However, some use is made of estimates of the changing distribution of wealth in a later chapter which attempts to provide quantitative bounds to the role of inheritance.[6]

It must not be forgotten too that the prime purpose of the work attempted here is to quantify the importance of inheritance in the *distribution of wealth*. Since the distribution is not constant over time, it is essential to take note of the changes that have occurred over the period under consideration or as much of the period as can be reasonably reliably estimated.

Many people believe that the existing data on the distribution of personal wealth in Britain are of rather poor quality compared to many other economic statistics (though unusually better perhaps than that of many other countries). The method of estimating the size distribution of personal wealth from that of those dying in any particular year was suggested in 1908 by Mallet[7] and the first estimates of any kind for Britain relate only to 1911. Hence recent data are more reliable and more complete than those of earlier years. From 1960 the Inland Revenue began to publish the official series of the distribution of personal wealth, and has continued to do so annually.

The Diamond Commission has discussed the Inland Revenue series at some length and has attempted to improve them in various ways. One of the most useful contributions the Commission has made from the point of view of this study is to draw attention to the sensitivity of the estimates of the distribution to differing assumptions that must be made in the process of estimation. These are fully documented in the Reports and in Atkinson and Harrison (1978) and need not be described in detail here. However, it is useful to point out that the need for such assumptions is largely due to two gaps in the coverage of the Inland Revenue statistics: these are usually referred to as the 'missing (or excluded) population' and 'missing wealth'.

The missing people are those persons who die with small amounts of wealth which do not therefore come to the attention of the Inland Revenue. No one knows exactly how many such people there are since the number of wealth holders depends on the age at which individuals start to hold wealth in their own right. However, we may be confident that they must be very large. In 1973, for example, the population covered in the Inland Revenue Statistics was 19 million as against 39 million in the total adult population of Britain aged 18 and over. Assumptions must therefore be made of the amount of wealth held by missing persons, and these can substantially affect the resulting estimates of inequality. Similarly, account must be taken of the categories of missing *wealth* which include specific assets like pension rights and trust property which are not part of the estate on which duty is paid and may not therefore come to the Inland Revenue's attention, and also of shortfalls in all asset categories (differences between totals obtained by different methods).

The effect of eight varying assumptions made by the Diamond Commission (1975) about missing people and missing wealth are shown in Table 1.1 in order to give some idea of the range of possible differences which arise in the field of wealth distribution estimation. The figures in the table, it must be remembered, relate to 1972 only. For much of the purposes to which these statistics are put, the need is for a series showing trends in wealth shares over time. One might hope therefore that series based on most of the different assumptions would move more or less in line, in the medium or long term.

Table 1.1 *Sensitivity of Estimates of Wealth Distribution to Alternative Assumptions, Great Britain, 1972*

Per Cent Shares of Percentiles on Assumptions 1–8 (see notes below)

	1	2	3	4	5	6	7	8
Top 1 per cent	29·9	28·1	28·8	26·8	23·7	30·8	25·6	17·4
2–5	26·4	25·8	26·4	24·6	20·9	28·2	24·5	17·5
6–10	15·6	13·4	13·8	12·7	11·9	15·0	13·8	10·8
11–20	17·3	15·1	15·4	14·5	14·1	16·3	16·9	13·6
21–100	10·8	17·6	15·6	21·4	29·4	9·7	19·2	40·7

Source: Royal Commission on the Distribution of Income and Wealth, Report No. 1, Initial Report on the Standing Reference (Cmnd 6171, 1975), pp. 87, 88 and 92.

Assumption 1 – Concentration of wealth among adult population, assuming excluded persons have no wealth.

2 – Allocating to the excluded and included population the difference in total wealth between estate duty multiplier totals and balance sheet totals.

3 – Persons excluded from the Inland Revenue Coverage have wealth of £500 per head.

4 – Wealth holding of excluded population is £1,000 per head.

5 – The difference between the estate duty multiplier totals and balance sheet totals is allocated to the excluded population.

6 – The difference between balance sheet and estate duty multiplier totals allocated to the included population.

7 – Wealth adjusted for balance sheet totals and including £20,000 million of occupational pension rights.

8 – As 7 but including also state pension rights.

Unfortunately such a set of different series covering the last hundred years whereby the hypothesis in the last paragraph can be put to the test is not available. The Inland Revenue data start in 1960 and for individual years before then there are independent estimates, most of which are for various reasons not comparable with each other. The only consistent series extending from 1972 back, though with some gaps, to 1923 is the very recent one by Atkinson and Harrison (1978). We make use of this in a number of places in this book. The main trends can be observed from Table 1.2. They show that there was a substantial decline in the share of the top 1 per cent in total personal wealth which was of the order of approximately ½ per cent per annum over the fifty-year period. Shares of the top 5, 10 and 20 percentiles fell very much less. Indeed the whole of the decline in the shares of the top groups below the top 1 per cent appears to be due to the trend in the top percentile. The share of the next richest 4 per cent of wealth holders in fact rose a little over the period taken as a whole, while the shares of the next highest percentage groups rose quite considerably. This evidence is in line with the view that the observed decline in inequality may reflect in large part a redistribution among the members of wealthy families. It therefore raises questions about the importance of inheritance over the period and of family wealth on which it is hoped that the results presented here throw some light.

Table 1.2 *Shares in Total Personal Wealth, England and Wales, 1923–72*

	Top 1%	Top 5%	Top 10%	Top 20%
1923	60·9	82·0	89·1	94·2
1924	59·9	81·5	88·1	93·8
1925	61·0	82·1	88·4	93·8
1926	57·3	79·9	87·4	93·2
1927	59·8	81·3	88·3	93·8
1928	57·0	79·6	87·2	93·1
1929	55·5	78·9	86·3	92·6
1930	57·9	79·2	86·6	92·6
1936	54·2	77·4	85·7	92·0
1938	55·0	76·9	85·0	91·2
1950	47·2	74·3	—	—
1951	45·8	73·6	—	—
1952	43·0	70·2	—	—
1953	43·6	71·1	—	—
1954	45·3	71·8	—	—
1955	44·5	71·1	—	—
1956	44·5	71·3	—	—
1957	43·4	68·7	—	—
1958	41·4	67·8	—	—
1959	41·4	67·6	—	—
1960	33·9	59·4	71·5	83·1
1961	36·5	60·6	71·7	83·3
1962	31·4	54·8	67·3	80·2
1963	Not available*			
1964	34·5	58·6	71·4	84·3
1965	33·0	58·1	71·7	85·5
1966	30·6	55·5	69·2	83·8
1967	31·4	56·0	70·0	84·5
1968	33·6	58·3	71·6	85·1
1969	31·1	56·1	67·7	83·3
1970	29·7	53·6	68·7	84·5
1971	28·4	52·3	67·6	84·2
1972	31·7	56·0	70·4	84·9

Source: Atkinson and Harrison (1978), p. 159.
Notes: — denotes outside range of estate duty statistics.

* The estate data were not available by country for 1963.

NOTES

1   Little and Fleming hung their case for a wealth tax for Britain heavily on the need to substitute capital taxes for those on investment income in order to encourage saving (Little and Fleming, 1974). Most recently the 'Meade Report' (1978) has also come out in favour of adding wealth to the tax base.

2   Curiously enough, perhaps, there seems to be a kind of conventional wisdom that regards wealth acquired by outright gambling to be exempt from taxation as far as the individual winner is concerned (though the revenues of football pools etc. are taxable).

3   One might, however, call attention to a recent argument pointing out the losses that may accrue to a society that diminishes inheritance of wealth but allows continuing concentration of power in government, trade unions and large corporations (Spearman, 1975).

4   Another reason is the need to estimate the importance of inheritance among women, for whom the same proxies are unlikely to be appropriate.

5   The tax concession to owner-occupiers buying their houses on mortgage may work to offset this.

6   Use is also made of estimates of the changing share of the top 10 per cent of the wealth distribution in the construction (see below) of an index which attempts to allow for changes in prices and distribution: see Chapter 3.

7   The method consists of taking the distribution of wealth among the dying as a sample of that among the whole population. If the numbers in each age/sex class are known the former can be estimated from the latter by using sets of so-called 'estate duty multipliers' which are defined as the reciprocals of the mortality rates for each age/sex class. Full explanations can be found in Atkinson and Harrison (1977).

2

The Nature of the Evidence

Despatch is the soul of business: and nothing contributes
more to despatch than method.

Lord Chesterfield:
A letter to his son, 5 February 1750

The quantification of inheritance in this study is achieved by comparing
the wealth left at death by different members of the same family. The
form in which the results will first be presented may be illustrated by
Table 2.1. This shows for a sample of sons dying in 1973 all of whom left
more than £200,000, the percentages who were preceded by fathers
leaving estates of different sizes. The method was first devised by
Wedgwood (1929) in a pioneering study in the 1920s. The work set out
here is modelled on his and is based on the analysis of a number of
samples of decedents drawn for each of the years 1902, 1924–6, 1956–7,
1965 and 1973.

This chapter is devoted to a description of the data and the methods
used to analyse them. It is long and to a considerable extent technical. It
was thought best to discuss these matters in some detail separately here
in order to allow for the presentation of the results of the study in as
straightforward a manner as possible. The chapter may therefore be
omitted by those who do not wish to concern themselves with the
methodology but only with the results. However, it must be pointed out
that the study covers a period of rather more than a hundred years,
during which time substantial changes have occurred. These are
reflected in the data, which have been subjected to treatment of various
kinds in order to make them as comparable as possible. Interpretation of
the results necessarily involves appreciation of the limitations imposed
by the data, but we have, of course, attempted to allow for all aspects of
this of which we are aware.

METHOD

The names of persons whose wills are probated and of certain others
who die intestate are listed alphabetically in the volumes of the
Calendars at the Central Probate Registry in Somerset House, London.
These have formed the basic data for the bulk of the research. The details
printed in the Calendars have varied a little over the years, but they

Table 2.1 *Estates of Fathers and Sons Dying in 1973 (current prices)*

| | | | | | *Cumulative percentages of total numbers of estates* | | | | | | |
| | | | | | *Father's Estate Size* | | | | | | |
Son's Estate Size £200,000 and over	*Over £1,000,000*	*Over £500,000*	*Over £250,000*	*Over £100,000*	*Over £50,000*	*Over £25,000*	*Over £10,000*	*Over £5,000*	*Over £1,000*	*All*	*Sample Size*
	2	4	9	25	37	47	60	70	77	100	112

Table 2.2 *The Samples of Wealth Leavers*

Sample No.	*Year*	*Number of Persons Sampled*	*Sex*	*Estate Range*	*Predecessor(s) or Successor(s)*	*Matched Tracing Relationship*
I	1973	122	male	£200,000 and over	Successors	Parents
II	1973	300	male	£15,000 to £200,000	Successors	Parents
III	1973	140	female	£200,000 and over	Successors	Parents
IV	1965	159	male	£100,000 and over	Successors	Parents
V	1956–7	590	male	£100,000 and over	Successors	Parents
VI	1956–7	95	male	£50,000 to £100,000	Successors	Parents
VII	1924–6	55	male	£200,000 and over	Predecessors+Successors	Parents+Children
VIII	1902	76	male	£100,000 and over	Predecessors	Children

Note: Names of persons in each sample are classified by the size of their estate at death.

include only minimum information about the name and address of the deceased, the gross value of his estate at death and other minor details. Their purpose is to help those who wish to examine the papers relating to a particular individual to find them. The documents available to any member of the public on payment of a search fee are a will, and the grant which authorises the executors or administrators to dispose of the assets belonging to the deceased. The will itself contains of course information about legacies and bequests. The grant, over some but not the entire period of the study, records also the *net* value of the estate, and the duty paid. In Scotland only, an additional document is available to the public – the affidavit listing separately all the assets of the estate.

Sampling Procedure
Sample names were drawn for various classes of wealth leavers as set out in Table 2.2. The sampling procedure assumes that those dying in any particular year are randomly drawn from the living population in any age/sex/social class group.[1] Samples were selected alphabetically by surname within each year. A–M for samples I, IV and VIII, though in the case of the last of these every twelfth name was selected to yield a sample of approximately $12\frac{1}{2}$ per cent, A and B for sample II – in *all* letters of the alphabet for the top wealth leavers of samples III, V, VI and VII.[23] Table 2.2 shows the year of each sample, the number and sex of the persons included and the estate size covered.

Samples of Successors and Predecessors
The final two columns of the table require special explanation. They identify the samples as being one of two types, determined by a simple characteristic. This is whether the matching process in the fieldwork involved searching for predecessors or for successors. Sample I, for example, is of men who died in 1973 and the research involved tracing their parents, or to be more specific, the sample was of sons who died in 1973 and the search was to trace their fathers. The sample of sons is therefore described as being of successors, or a *backward tracing* sample. Samples II to VI inclusive are also the backward tracing type.

In contrast, sample VIII consists of men who died in 1902 and the fieldwork involved searching for and tracing their children, in particular their sons. It is therefore described as a *forward tracing* sample and the men of 1902 are regarded as predecessors.

It will be noted that sample VII[4] is shown as being both forward and backward tracing. The decedents of that year who formed the sample acted as a bridge, as it were, between the other two types. The searching for them was both forward, tracing their sons and backward, tracing their fathers. Hence there were in this case three generations of families about whose wealth we have evidence.

There are a number of reasons for distinguishing between the first type of samples of successors, such as sons, where fathers are traced, and the second type of samples of predecessors such as fathers, where sons are traced. The most important difference is that each helps to answer different questions. The former provides evidence about such questions as what proportion of rich persons who died in a certain year were preceded by rich parents or were self-made? In contrast, the second type of sample helps answer the rather different type of question of what proportion of rich men who died in a given year were succeeded by children who increased, maintained or dissipated their fortunes?

Top Wealth Leavers

Particular interest attaches in a study of inheritance to individuals at the top of the wealth distribution. Our samples were drawn with this in mind and we identify a group described as Top Wealth Leavers (TWL) for special examination and analysis. TWL are defined as those leaving approximately sufficient wealth to place them in the top 0·1 per cent of wealth holders. The largest TWL sample is for the year 1956–7, when the minimum wealth needed to qualify for inclusion in the top 0·1 per cent was approximately £100,000. For the most recent sample of 1973 the minimum qualifying sum for TWL was £200,000 which amount also roughly put a person in the top 0·1 per cent of the distribution. Although it may seem that ownership of wealth of £200,000 in 1973 is on the small side to call oneself really wealthy, about 30,000 persons in that year were estimated to possess wealth in excess of this amount.

Men and Women in the Samples

Another characteristic shown in Table 2.2 is the sex of decedents, the bulk of which are male. However, it was thought important to examine separately the importance of inheritance among rich women and even more interestingly perhaps, the extent of intermarriage among the wealthy. For this reason sample III was drawn of 140 top female wealth leavers and attempts were made to trace the estates of the three persons from whom they might have been particularly likely to inherit – their fathers, husbands and fathers-in-law.

A related aspect of the study is that the main emphasis of the research, following Wedgwood, has been in the association between the wealth of fathers and that of sons. However, inheritances obviously occur also through other, less direct, lines. One cannot hope to cover all possible sources. But non-paternal wealth is treated in this study in two ways. First, it was possible to look for evidence of wealth acquired through marriage and the search for fathers-in-law, for the 1973 sample of women was extended also for the sample of male TWL of the same year. The wealth left at death by the mothers of the latter sample was also traced. The second method of looking at non-paternal sources of wealth was to take wealthy families and to construct what might be described as family wealth trees.

THE MATCHING PROCESS

Having selected the samples, the major task of the fieldwork was to match the estate of each individual in the sample with the relevant predecessor or successor. For example, in the case of the sample of persons dying in 1973, the need was to trace the estates of their fathers; in the case of the sample of decedents of 1902, the tracing required was of their sons.

The process is best illustrated by examining it from the point of view of searching for the estate of the father of a person in, say, the 1973 sample. Three essentially separate stages were involved: (1) identifying the father's *name*, (2) finding his *date of death*, and (3) tracing the value of his *estate* at death in the Probate Calendars. Three main methods of achieving the objective were employed: (a) by using biographical directories, (b) by searching in the General Registry of Births, Deaths and Marriages in St Catherine's House, London, and the Probate Registry itself, and (c) by correspondence with relatives, executors and friends of decedents.

The major directories employed in the searches were *Burke's Peerage*, *Debrett's*, *Burke's Landed Gentry*, *Who's Who*, *Kelly's Directory of the Titled, Landed and Official Classes*, but many other specialised and local biographical dictionaries also proved useful. Personal details in these source books usually include father's name, and occasionally also father's date of death. In the latter cases the tracing of father's estate was swiftly completed. Where only father's name was recorded it was necessary to institute a search for up to eighty years in the volumes of the Probate Calendars. A third of the 1956–7 sample of top male wealth leavers appeared in the directories cited. By 1973 the proportion had fallen to rather less than a fifth.

Searches in the General Registry Office of Births, Deaths and Marriages (GRO)

For persons who were not listed in any biographical directory, the searching process was much lengthier. The procedure was as follows:

(i)   Obtain the date of death of the person in the sample. This is recorded in the Probate Calendars.
(ii)   Identify his death entry in the index of deaths at the GRO and from his death certificate extract details of his date of birth.
(iii)   Search for his birth entry in the GRO and extract his father's name, address, occupation and his mother's first and maiden names from his birth certificate.
(iv)   Return to the Probate Registry and search for the estate of his father in the Probate Calendars.

The searching process for individual cases ranged from the straightforward to the complex. The chief determinant of the ease of tracing was whether the names involved were common or rare. Common names like John Walker led to immense difficulties at all stages, above all in the identification of the correct birth certificate. In these cases several possible birth entries came to light. This was a particular problem in samples drawn before 1970, after which time a change was made in the details reported on death from the deceased's 'age at death' to his 'date of birth'. For deaths prior to 1970, it was necessary to calculate the approximate year of birth, which could only limit the searching to a minimum of one year, even if accurately reported.[5]

Almost all those difficult cases involving multiple birth entries caused disproportionate amounts of fieldwork time. However, it was realised that persons with very common names would hardly be representative of the samples as a whole so far as the chance of having a rich father was concerned. To minimise bias in the results, therefore, extensive efforts were made to trace the fathers in these cases. Where several possible fathers came to light from such multiple birth entries searches were made for all of them in the Probate Calendars. It was sometimes possible to identify the correct entry by reference to fathers' wills – cross checking with sons' wills for addresses, mothers'/widows' names, the names of brothers, sisters, uncles etc. An alternative method used to identify the correct father was to search for the son's marriage certificate. This was very time consuming because one could only guess as a rule at the date of marriage, and it was only carried out when the son's will referred by name to his wife. In such cases, it must be added, a certain amount of judgement was necessary before a pair of estates could be adjudged correct with sufficient confidence to be included in the analysis. Most of the failures were in this category.

Correspondence and Other Means of Tracing Predecessors' Estates
Between a half and two-thirds of predecessors' estates were traced through the Probate Calendars with the help of information from directories or by lengthier searching in the GRO. The remaining successful searches were achieved by diverse means. A few came to light through obituary and other notices in local newspapers; a few more where a family business was involved, through searching for the disappearance of a director's name in the records at the Companies Registry; yet others through searches for other relatives in the GRO, and a small number by unorthodox means such as visiting local churchyards to identify gravestones.

However, by far the most important means of tracing estates in this category was a result of correspondence with relatives and other associates of the deceased (both for the whole sample and especially for self-made men with common names). This method was, in the event, so important as a means of tracing parental estates that it merits a brief account.

Almost 600 letters were dispatched relating to some 400 estates. Nearly half were to relatives, and a similar proportion to solicitors. The remaining 8 per cent went to a wide variety of persons, e.g. ministers, churchyard superintendents, local libraries, former employers, and employees etc. Almost two-thirds of the replies proved helpful – a somewhat remarkable result, given the prevailing conventional wisdom of the kind of co-operation one receives from inquiries about the rich. They led, moreover, to predecessors' estates being traced in about 70 per cent of cases and materially raised the success rate for the study as a whole.[6]

It was realised from the outset that the response rate to letters from those associated with self-made men might differ from that about men with rich fathers. There could therefore be a bias introduced into the results, the nature of which is difficult to predict. For this reason analysis was undertaken of response rates by different classes both of addressee and of decedent. In particular, tests were made between response rates for different sizes of fathers' and of sons' estates, broken down by those sent to relatives, those to solicitors and for each of the samples.

Analysis by wealth size class showed a higher response rate for associates of top wealth leavers than for those with smaller estates. Slightly less co-operation was also received where wealth had been inherited than where fortunes were self-made. The results also show that helpful response rates did not differ very much between relatives and solicitors, though they rose marginally for the former between the 1950s and 1970s while they fell slightly for solicitors over the same period.

A remarkable feature of the correspondence was the very low level of antagonism expressed about the inquiry. Only 3 per cent of addressees wrote that they were unwilling to help – 2 per cent because they objected to the nature of the research.[7] The rest were solicitors and executors who stated that they regarded it to be a breach of the relationship with their clients to disclose information, even though publicly available. This is in marked contrast, incidentally, to the attitude taken by the majority of solicitors, many of whom freely searched their files for us and sometimes even supplied confidential, if not sensitive, supplementary information about their clients.[8] It is true that some non-respondents may not have wished to help. On the other hand many letters may not have reached recipients, where they were, by association, of the same generation as the deceased. Moreover, the number of persons gratuitiously offering additional and unsolicited background information about the sources of wealth of the decedents far exceeded the letters received objecting to the inquiry. A number of respondents put themselves to a good deal of trouble trying to get the information we required on our behalf from other relatives. People sent us potted biographies, family trees, wills and even came to see us bringing copies of financial accounts kept over very long periods. We talked to a few of the more forthcoming respondents and rarely failed to acquire valuable information.[9]

SMALL ESTATES NOT IN THE PROBATE CALENDARS

A word should be said about the estates of those identified mainly through correspondence with relatives which turned out to be too small to be listed in the Probate Registry. In such cases dates of death were often supplied leading to the identification of an entry in the Register of Deaths. If, however, no estate was listed in the Probate Calendar, reliance was placed on the occupation of the deceased recorded on the death certificate. If this was menial, e.g. labourer, it was assumed that the estate was indeed small. In a very few cases the practice of relying on the word of the correspondent was adopted if it was to the effect that the person in question 'left very little'. On the other hand where there was no date of death or the occupation was suspect (e.g. fur trader) the case was regarded as a failure because the individual might have died abroad, and both father and son were omitted from the analysis. Wherever an estate was confidently regarded as being too small to be listed in the Probate Registry, it was entered on the data tapes at an arbitrary nominal value of £50.

SUCCESS RATES

In view of the virtual absence of information about the quantitative importance of inheritance and the fact that sons with wealthy fathers were highly likely to be more easily traced than those who were self-made, it was decided to strive for very high success rates. The size of the first sample searched – that for 1956–7 – was also particularly large because it was intended to provide some guidance on how to select later samples. This meant that the entire searching procedure was very protracted, largely because the difficulty attached to tracing estates tends to increase progressively as those listed in the directories and those with less and less uncommon names are found.

In the event, the success rates in tracing fathers' estates turned out to be very high. The rates were calculated after eliminating foreigners and men who had predeceased their fathers, but including those with small estates not in the Calendars but identified reliably as explained in the previous section. The success rates for the 1956–7, 1965 and 1973 samples were minimally about 95 per cent, though if one excludes a number of suspect foreigners and less reliable predecessors they are as high as 98 per cent. The lowest rates were for the 1973 sample of women wealth leavers. In the cases of the 1902 and 1924–6 samples the success rates are not easily calculable because we cannot be certain that all children of a family had been identified if not mentioned in a will. Some might also appear as 'failures' because they were still living. Our best estimates, however, put the success rates for the forward working samples barely lower than those for the forward tracing ones.[10]

NATURE AND RELIABILITY OF WEALTH DATA

The value of the approach adopted here to estimate the importance of inheritance must depend in part on the nature and reliability of the best data that is available on the wealth of individuals. Before entering into an extended discussion of data reliability and how it has changed over the period covered in the study, it is important to note certain characteristics of the nature of the data itself.

Nature of Wealth Data and Inheritance
It was argued in the previous chapter (p.4) that there is no single

unambiguous concept of wealth that is applicable to all situations. However, given the aim of this study with regard to the quantification of inheritance, it is possible to say something about the kind of data which would be best suited to this particular purpose. The ideal measure for any individual would be the sum total of all acquisitions of wealth received by him or her over his lifetime including gifts and legacies, of money and of money's worth, from fathers, husbands, fathers-in-law, other relatives, friends and acquaintances. It is hardly necessary to point out that such complete information is not at present available.[11] Therefore this study has had to make use of proxy measures, which are the values of estates left at death by fathers and, in a number of cases, also by other relatives. The proxy measures are of course not ideal. A son's inheritance differs from his father's wealth at death in so far as it is affected by the way in which the father distributes his property among his children and other beneficiaries, the number of his brothers and sisters, the value of gifts received during his lifetime etc.

Considerable effort was expended in trying to obtain information from wills about the size of individual legacies. This proved so difficult in so many cases that it was decided to base the analysis here on the estates left at death by two generations of the same family (making allowance in certain cases for family size).[12] While the data inevitably depart from the ideal, we do not feel that their limitations are so serious as to prevent the reaching of relevant conclusions. Father's wealth and son's inheritance may not be identical but they are likely to be highly correlated. However, the very special meaning given to the measure of inheritance employed here must not be overlooked in the interpretation of the results of this study.

Reliability of the Data. It is important to examine next the reliability of the data about the wealth of matched pairs of individuals from the same families. It has already been argued that the alphabetical sampling process is random. We have no reason to believe that there are any obvious important biases built into the data, other than those connected with the actual monetary valuation of estates,[13] which are now considered.

Tax Avoidance. It must be explained that the estate values used throughout the study are the gross values at death as admitted for probate. These values are known to be unreliable in a number of respects associated with the fact that the moment of a man's death is not necessarily a representative time at which to count up his capital. If he has indulged in tax avoidance and/or evasion in anticipation of death this will be particularly true, though it is possible to estimate some of the effects of this. For example, gifts *inter vivos* have probably been the most common form of death duty planning, and where a man has given away property instead of leaving it to be distributed in accordance with his will at death, a breakdown by age of decedents can be carried out in order to throw light on its quantitative importance.[14] The introduction of capital transfer tax on gifts may have lowered the incentive to give wealth away to children for tax reasons, but it does not affect this study, the data for which all precede 1974.

Discretionary Trusts. Other sources of concern about the reliability of probate valuations stem from the use of complex and sophisticated death duty avoidance techniques. These have changed, as has the law, over the years, but one device which is widely believed to have been of major importance has been the discretionary trust.[15] Very little is known about the extent of the use made by individuals of discretionary trusts in tax planning. Since the person setting up the trust loses complete and direct control over the assets he puts into the trust, they are not without drawbacks, particularly for those who do not have faith in their children or their trustees to carry out what they would have done themselves. However, for the very rich, they have been an obvious means of dramatically reducing liability to death duties.[16]

Tax Evasion

Illegal tax evasion as well as legal tax avoidance also, of course, reduces tax liability. It is difficult to estimate the quantitative importance of the deliberate concealment of the existence of property or of the under-reporting of its value. However, it seems likely that evasion will be relatively more important for small estates than for very large ones. Hiding a few bank notes and undervaluing personal effects in an estate of a thousand pounds seems inherently more feasible than a pro-portionately equivalent understatement in an estate of one million pounds.

Probate and Inland Revenue Valuations

Most of the published statistical information about the distribution of wealth is based on values declared by executors and administrators to the Inland Revenue (henceforth referred to as IR), for the purpose of meeting tax obligations. Both IR and probate values suffer from the deficiencies mentioned in the last section. It must now be said, however, that the probate valuations suffer certain additional disadvantages and that most of these tend to *under*state the value of the wealth of an individual. The formal difference between probate and IR valuations is that the former is intended to cover all those assets which an executor must dispose of in accordance with the testator's will (or according to the intestacy rules). The Inland Revenue valuation, on the other hand, covers all assets which must be included in the estate in order to assess tax liability on death.

The IR and probate valuations may be the same, and in the case of many small estates undoubtedly are so.[17] But sometimes the probate valuation is notably the smaller. This occurs, as indicated above, because probate is granted only for property that the decedent was legally empowered to distribute. The main type of asset that a man may have, but over which he does not have any power of disposal is an interest in property settled in trust by someone else from which he benefits during his lifetime. However, if the settler of the trust has already decided that the beneficial interest should pass to someone else on the death of the first beneficiary, the latter cannot bequeath his interest to anyone else. A common form of trust for a man to make is to leave property in trust for his wife to live on the income during her lifetime and, on her death, for the capital to pass to his children. The trust deeds may even specify that the capital shall pass to his grandchildren on the death of his children. In such cases the wife and the children have no power of disposal over the trust property. However, unless the trust is of the discretionary type described above, its value is part of the estate of the decedent for the purposes of estate duty – the proportion of the capital value deemed to pass on the death of a beneficiary depending on the share he had in the trust fund when he was alive. This dutiable trust property is included in Inland Revenue data and not in probate valuations.

A Statistical Comparison of Probate and IR Valuations

The only source of information about the wealth of *named individuals*, and therefore of matched fathers and sons, available to the general public is the Probate Calendars. It is therefore of some importance to compare probate and IR valuations. Such comparisons are helped by the publication by the IR of the distribution of estates passing on death each year. No similar statistics are published of probate values. However, the Probate Calendars have themselves been produced on a computer since 1974 and a size distribution was kindly run specially for this research. It is shown below in Table 2.3, set alongside the closest comparable figures of the IR. Differences in coverage between the probate and IR bases of the statistics to be noted are: (i) the former relate to the calendar year 1974 and the latter to the fiscal year 1973/4; (ii) both are restricted theoretically to England and Wales; (iii) the former are gross and the latter net capital values (see below, pp.23 and 26).

It can be seen that the overall totals are tolerably close. Using probate valuations there is a deficiency of about 5 per cent by both number and capital value of estates compared with Inland Revenue. However, the shortfall is much greater in the highest size classes of estates. There are about a third fewer estates in the £50,000 to £100,000 category, about a half in the £100,000 to £200,000 and about two-thirds in the highest category of all, £200,000 and over.[18]

In view of the special interest in this study in top wealth leavers and the absence of further details in the computer print-out supplied to us of the distribution of probate values, we arranged for samples to be drawn from the Calendars of larger estates for 1973 and 1974, broken down by sex and size. The tabulations are relegated to Appendix A. They show that probate valuations understate women's estates compared to men's, due doubtless to the fact that women have a higher proportion held in trust for them during their lives. A further difference between probate and IR valuations in Table 2.3 which was mentioned above is that the

Table 2.3   A Comparison of Probate and Inland Revenue Valuations, Numbers and Capital Values of Estates, England and Wales, 1974

| Lower Limit of Capital Value | Numbers | | Capital Values (£000s) | |
	Probated Estates	Inland Revenue Estates	Gross Probate Values	Net Inland Revenue Values
Nil	42,986	48,996	27,568	25,900
£1,000	68,378	62,440	123,224	113,764
£3,000	31,328	34,385	122,677	136,452
£5,000	54,821	63,276	403,258	469,105
£10,000	62,258	61,690	922,712	926,402
£25,000	13,707	15,012	463,388	524,210
£50,000	4,437	5,985	298,984	392,637
£100,000	1,266	1,969	168,347	258,330
£200,000	398	652	207,633	280,080
Total ALL	279,579	294,405	2,737,791	3,126,880

Sources: (1) Probate Registry – privately supplied by officials at the Central Probate Registry; (2) Inland Revenue statistics (1975).

former are measured *gross* while the latter are *net*, i.e. after deduction of funeral expenses and debts due to the estates. Net probate values are not given in the Calendars, though they are currently available from the document granting administration to executors.[19] Tabulations of the distributions according to probate valuations for estates of £100,000 and over in the Appendix also distinguish between gross and net estates. The net values show, as would be expected, a greater deficiency compared with the IR figures than the gross probate values. The extra shortfall is not however very great. For the average of the years 1973–4, the number of estates with probated values of £100,000 and over was 1,685 *gross* compared with 1,502 *net*.[20]

The broad conclusion that must be drawn from the somewhat technical but important foregoing discussion is that probate values tend to underestimate the real value of a person's estate, particularly for the largest estate classes and for women. There is, however, no alternative to using probate values for the kind of work on the quantification of inheritance undertaken here.[21] The nature of the biases to be expected must however be clearly understood so that the statistical results of the research may be properly interpreted.

Further Tests of the Accuracy of Probate Valuations
In addition to setting the probate and IR data for particular years side by side for comparative purposes two further tests of the accuracy of probate valuations were made, one using additional data on settled dutiable property provided by the Inland Revenue and one quite independent.

Settled Dutiable Property
The extent to which the deficiency between probate and IR valuations is due to the absence of settled dutiable property can be independently assessed. The Estate Duty Office (as it then was) made available to us for the years 1956–7 additional breakdowns giving the total value of settled property on which duty was paid for estates of £100,000 and over. The data showed a 26 per cent deficiency in the proportion of settled to total property in the IR statistics comparable with those for 1956–7 and 1974 (see Table 2.3 and Harbury, 1962, p. 848).

For later years the Diamond Commission (1977) carried out a survey of the relative importance of trust property to 'free' estate in 1973. They show the ratio of dutiable to free estate for estates classified by size. The full results are tabulated in Table 2.4.

The results show rather lower proportions than in the earlier years for the samples the Commission drew. It can be seen also that the relative importance of non-free property, not surprisingly falls substantially with estate size and is only 6·4 per cent for those in the £15,000 to £50,000 class.

Property Millionaires
The magnitude of the wealth of the living is often referred to in the press

Table 2.4 *Size of Non-free and Free Estates Broken Down by Estate Size Class, 1973*

Range of total Estate (before duty)	Average Values				
	Free Estate £	Non-free Estate £	Total Estate £	Proportion of non-free estate to total estate %	Sample Size*
£500,000 and over	910,839	215,384	1,126,233	19·1	—
£100,000 and under £500,000	174,693	25,581	200,274	12·8	—
£50,000 and under £100,000	64,462	5,277	69,740	7·6	—
£15,000 and under £50,000	26,586	1,832	28,417	6·4	—
All estates	308,311	65,115	373,426		238

Source: Royal Commission on the Distribution of Income and Wealth, Report No. 5, p. 280.
* A breakdown of sample sizes by estate range is not given.

and elsewhere. The basis of such statements as appear from time to time, for example, in *Fortune* is not always clearly stated, but it usually involves an assessment of the value of assets such as company stock known, or believed to be held, by an individual or his family. Ten years ago a list of 100 men stated to be millionaires was published by Oliver Marriott.[22] Several of them were already dead and it was a fair guess that others would have died by the time this research was under way. It was therefore decided to search through the Probate Calendars to see the size of their wealth at death. The outcome was that the estates of 22 of Marriott's millionaires were discovered. Their names and the values of their estate are given in Appendix B, while the distribution is summarised in Table 2.5. The results are of some interest and, to an extent, encouraging. As can be seen a third of Marriott's sample actually left free estate valued at over a million pounds (the largest being over £12 million). More significant it may be argued is the fact that all but one of the twenty-two left estates worth more than £100,000; the remaining individual left approximately £70,000.

Marriott does not give individual estimates of the wealth of his millionaires when they were alive.[23] No very precise comparisons of the accuracy of probate valuations could, therefore, be made even if one could estimate the fall in property values and other changes which must have occurred between the time of Marriott's estimates and the dates of death of the men in his list. But because all but one of Marriott's samples left more than £100,000, the important conclusion emerges that samples drawn with a minimum wealth at that figure are likely to include most millionaires. Further, since this was approximately the lower limit of the

Table 2.5   *Probate Values of the Estates of Twenty-Four 'Property Millionaires' (current prices)*

Cumulative percentages of the total number of estates				
Over £1m.	*Over £½m.*	*Over £¼m.*	*Over £100,000*	*Over £50,000*
36	50	73	95	100

definition of Top Wealth Leavers in this study, it suggests that the Top Wealth *Leavers* sampled here may not have been unrepresentative of the top wealth *holders* in the population. For without intending to suggest that the millionaires of the property boom of the sixties were any more likely than any other group of the very rich to engage in tax avoidance, few people would probably regard them as having a significantly lower propensity to avoid taxes than the average.

An Assessment of the Reliability of Probate Valuations
Having regard to all the evidence in the foregoing section on the reliability of probate valuations, we should say that it is our considered view that the sampling procedures for top wealth leavers have caught the great majority of the really wealthy in the age (and alphabetical) groups for the years selected. This statement is in no way intended to imply that the probate valuations in individual cases, particularly at the top of the distribution, are to be regarded as giving a reliable indication of their wealth.

INTERTEMPORAL DIFFERENCES IN THE DATA

The previous section has dealt with the general problems relating to the use of probate valuations. The next task is to consider how far the changes which have taken place in the period covered by the study cause difficulties in achieving comparability over time.

Realty and Personalty
English law distinguishes between realty and personalty, the former corresponding broadly to 'immovable' property like land and houses, and the latter to other 'moveables' like personal effects and stocks and shares. The first point to make is that probate valuations prior to 1894 were restricted to personalty and did not extend to real estate. Wedgwood, in his study of the wealth of the fathers of his sample of decedents of the 1920s, had to face this problem, though for him it was much more acute since the proportion of the fathers of his sample who died before 1894 was quite high. Wedgwood's solution was to make use of the data in the Returns of Landowners compiled by the Local Government Boards in the 1870s to add estimates of realty to the probate figures of personalty in appropriate cases.[24] The same solution was adopted in this study, though the numbers of cases involved was

very much smaller, 15 per cent of the total in 1956–7, falling to less than 5 per cent in the later samples.

Gross Versus Net Values

It was earlier pointed out that the probate valuations of estates used in this study are based on *gross* rather than net amounts, after deduction of funeral expenses and debts due on the estate. It is arguable that it might have been preferable to take probate valuations net of both debts and of duty paid on the estate, though for reasons to be explained shortly this is not necessarily the case. However, the figures of net values of estates on the grants of administration include realty and personalty only since 1947. Likewise duty paid on estates is recorded on the grant only since 1934. In consequence, in order to maintain comparability over the whole period of the study, gross values were used throughout.[25] However, this does not mean that gross values are necessarily inferior to net ones. It has already been shown that the exclusion of settled property causes probate values to understate net wealth, and there are other circumstances which give reason for thinking that for the wealthy, in at least a number of cases, the gross probate valuation represents a better indication of a decedent's live net worth. Gifts *inter vivos* are probably the main reason, but one also wonders when one sees an estate valued at £100,000 gross, net nil, whether a beggar can incur debts of £100,000.[26]

Success Rates

A second set of reasons why it might be important to examine the comparability of the data over time is related to changing success rates in tracing predecessors' or successors' estates. These could, in principle, be serious if they affected the observed proportions of self-made men to those with inherited wealth in the results. There are three aspects to be considered, related to success in identifying birth entries in the GRO, to correspondence with relatives and to the use made of wills reported in *The Times*.

Changes in the GRO. As mentioned earlier (pp.15, 16), a change took place in 1970 in the details required to be reported on registration of a death. Before then the requirement was for the *age* at death of the deceased; after that date it was for his *date of birth*. Because births are filed in quarterly volumes and because reporters usually seem to get birthdays right, the new information provided a much more powerful means of identification, so that success rates in GRO searching tended to be higher for the 1973 samples than for those of earlier years. Moreover, the higher success rates would almost certainly bias the results derived from the 1973 samples in favour of higher proportions of self-made men simply because the most difficult cases to trace were of persons with very common names.

The problem was not of very great magnitude because the sample of top wealth leavers for 1973 was only of limited size. It was, however, decided to test for possible bias by excluding from the 1973 data those pairs of fathers and sons who were adjudged unlikely to have been traced previously without the exact date of birth. This was to some extent an arbitrary matter, but six fathers were eliminated because their ages suggested at least seven possible birth entries.[27]

Correspondence. Success rates in tracing estates are affected by rates of favourable response from those to whom letters were sent asking for assistance. There were two kinds of change that took place over the period. The first relates to response rates in the three most recent sample years, 1956–7, 1965 and 1973. These did not in fact vary greatly, being 64 per cent, 60 per cent and 58 per cent respectively. However, it so happened that the decline in rates over time was approximately offset by a change in research policy, involving the sending of a higher proportion of letters in 1973 than in previous years. Hence it was felt that any remaining bias was likely to be too small to cause concern.

The second change that should be noted is that no letters at all were sent in connection with the two forward tracing samples, of persons dying in 1902 and 1924–6, for the obvious reason that the information from their wills about relatives was too far out of date to make such efforts worthwhile. However, largely no doubt because the samples were all of top wealth leavers, the success rates were not significantly lower for these than for the other samples. Hence it was again felt justifiable to ignore any resulting bias on this score.

Wills Not Registered in The Times. A final source of sampling error of importance relates to the data of 1924–6 only. This was the sample taken first by Wedgwood, but which is also used here. The main difference between this sample and others is that the original list of names was taken from different sources. Wedgwood's names were taken from the lists of wills published in *The Times*, whereas the others were drawn directly from the Calendars at the Probate Registry. The possibility of the results being biased in the direction of showing a higher proportion of men with inherited wealth arises because the probability that the self-made were less likely to have their wills reported in *The Times* is real enough for some attempt being made to quantify it. A test was therefore made with estates of £100,000 and over in the 1956–7 sample, which had been drawn from the Calendars. It was then discovered that the wills of approximately 90 per cent of the decedents had been reported in *The Times*.

While it was not possible to allow completely for any resulting bias, it was felt that some assessment of its quantitative importance should be gained. The procedure followed was, therefore, to analyse separately the relationship between the estates of those matched fathers and sons of the 1956–7 sample who were not reported in *The Times* and to contrast them with the overall results. Table 2.6 has been constructed with this objective. It employs a rough measure of the importance of inheritance by using a bench-mark based on the ratio of son's estate to father's estate. The table shows the proportions of sons in each estate size class

whose estates were valued for probate in 1956–7 at more than six times
that of their fathers. These proportions can be compared with the
proportions of all estates possessing this characteristic, also given in the
table. The figures in the table appear to confirm the hypothesis that the
exclusion of cases in the 1924–6 sample not reported in *The Times* did
impart a bias favouring those with inherited wealth as against the self-
made. This seems likely to have been greatest in the estate size class
£100,000 to £200,000 where the proportions of sons preceded by fathers
with estates less than one-sixth of their own was 53 per cent for those *not*
in *The Times* compared to 41 per cent for the whole sample. Some
attempt to allow for this bias was made by excluding estates not in *The
Times* in a separate analysis comparing the sample of that year with
Wedgwood's data for 1924–6.[28]

Table 2.6   *Wills Not Reported in* The Times, *1956–7*

Size of Son's Estate	Ratio $\dfrac{Son's\ Estate}{Father's\ Estate} > 6$		Numbers of Estates	
	NIT	*All*	*NIT*	*All*
	per cent of Row totals			
£500,000 and over	100	54	1	26
£300,000 and under £500,000	50	51	4	41
£200,000 and under £300,000	83	46	6	72
£100,000 and under £200,000	53	41	53	391

NIT = Not reported in *The Times.*

Changes in the Price Level
Research into intergenerational wealth transfers involves comparisons
of wealth over periods of time – in the case of this study of more than 100
years – over which prices are changing. It follows that attempts must be
made to render money values at different points of time as comparable
as possible. The usual method of making allowance for price changes is
by the use of index numbers.

The problem of choosing an appropriate index number to derive
estate values at constant prices leads immediately to the realisation that
there is not even an ideal theoretical index number that should be
employed. This is because prices do not all move in line with one another
and because there is no unique characteristic of wealth that should be
allowed for. Wealth may be held for several reasons and unless the
motive is known one cannot decide on the most appropriate way to

adjust the data collected at different times. It may be suggested that wealth may be held for three basically different motives (or a mixture of them) and that each may apply to an individual whether he inherits or accumulates wealth.

(1) *Consumption motive*, i.e. to spend the proceeds on goods and services.
(2) *Retention motive*, i.e. to hold assets in order, for example, to pass them on to the next generation.
(3) *Income motive*, i.e. to hold assets in order specifically to derive an income from them.

It is argued that a different index is needed for each case. For example, in the case of the consumption motive the assumption is that the wealth will be used to spend on consumer goods and services and the appropriate index is that which shows the course of retail prices. In the case of the retention motive, wealth holders are assumed to wish to retain their wealth (e.g. to pass it on to the next generation) and the prices that must be held constant are those of the assets that they hold. In the final case, of the income motive, the assumption is that people hold wealth only to derive an income from it. For them the proper index is one of asset yields; though if the income is required to be spent on goods and services, an index of retail prices should also be incorporated.

The price index of consumer goods and services was the only index used over the entire period. In order to minimise revaluation for the large sample in 1956–7, the average of those two years was chosen as the base. Hence estates for all years are expressed in constant 1956–7 prices.

For other indices there were no existing series extending far enough back to be of use. Two weighted average index numbers going back to 1900 were therefore specially constructed. Full details of both are given in Appendix C.

The asset price index followed the principles used in Sandford's index (Sandford and Wright, 1969). Price series were collected for each of the major class of assets in the Inland Revenue statistics. Weighted average indices should then ideally have been applied to each individual estate, according to the relative importance of each asset in its portfolio. However, the asset structure of individual estates in England and Wales is not known. In the absence of this information, use was made of the Inland Revenue statistics of the asset composition of estates by sex and size class. These were taken as the bases on which the weights applicable to any estate in any given year should be calculated. The yield price index was conceptually very similar to the asset price index, except that the yields on consols formed the basis for the index. For full details see Appendix C.

Relative Wealth Index. A final different approach to the problem of standardising for changes in the price level has also been adopted. This is to hold constant, not the real value of the assets, their yield or purchasing power, but the relative position of an estate of a given size in the size distribution of personal wealth as a whole.[29] The reason for doing this may be illustrated by considering two wealth leavers, both of whom had fathers who left £25,000. Father A died in year 1 and father B twenty years later in year 20. The normal way of standardising for changing prices is to use a price index number to express the wealth of fathers A and B in terms of constant prices. But in addition to the changes that took place in the price level between years 1 and 2, suppose that the distribution of wealth also became more equal. It might then be of interest to compare the wealth of the two fathers in the light of the position each had in the distribution of wealth. For even if the price level had not changed, it is possible that an estate of £25,000 would put a man in, say, the top 20 per cent of the distribution in year 1 and only in the top 50 per cent in year 2.

An index number was therefore devised to reflect the changing distribution of wealth over the years since 1900. The basis for the index could, of course, be any parameter of the distribution of wealth, such as the gini coefficient, mean or median wealth or the share of any given percentile. The decision was taken to use as base the minimum wealth needed by an individual in the years from 1900 to 1973 to secure a place in the top 10 per cent of the distribution. The series of figures of minimum wealth used were estimated from Atkinson and Harrison (1978) data (extrapolated from 1923 back to 1900). Details of the method of construction of the relative wealth and other indices are contained in Appendix C.

Figure 2.1 displays the movements of the various index numbers used to render the values of the estates of fathers and sons more comparable. Their implications are discussed in Chapter 3.

METHODS OF ANALYSIS

The last matter to be dealt with in this chapter is to explain the methods of analysis that are used to quantify inheritance. It is useful here to distinguish two separate issues, one concerned with statistical techniques and the other with the chief types of tabulations to which the techniques are applied.

Statistical Techniques

The first method of comparing the wealth of different generations of the same family is simply to relate the one to the other in a cumulative frequency table, such as that which appears at the beginning of this chapter. These can show, for example, the percentages of a group of wealth leavers who were preceded by fathers who left more than various amounts of wealth. If fathers' and sons' wealth are all expressed in constant prices, these percentages can be understood to be in real, rather than money terms. Considerable reliance is placed in Chapters 3 to 5 on tables of this kind.

The tabulations referred to in the previous paragraph relate to

Figure 2.1 *A graphical comparison of the relationship between four price indices, 1900–73 (base year 1956–7)*

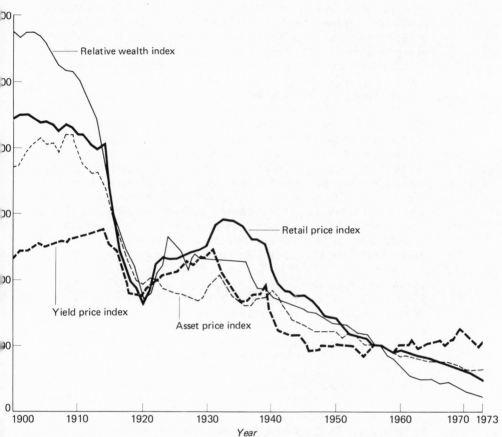

Note: The index numbers are those used to inflate estates of those dying before 1956–7 (and to deflate estates of those dying after 1956–7) in order to value them at the prices ruling in the average of those years. For example, an estate valued at £100,000 in 1920, when the index was 200, would be revalued at £200,000 in 1956–7 prices.

inheritance and the accumulation of fortunes rather than to their dissipation. They are associated, therefore, with the so-called 'backward tracing' samples, where the fathers and other predecessors of the wealth leavers of 1956–7, 1965 and 1973 were sought. For the 'forward tracing' samples, the estates sought were those of the sons of the wealth leavers of 1902 and 1924–6. In these latter cases it was thought sensible to make some allowance for differences in family size before comparing the estates of fathers and sons. This was done by dividing each father's estate by both the number of his sons and by that of the total number of his children.[30]

Growth Rates. A second measure used in the analysis introduces time into the comparisons. An attempt is made to incorporate the time span between the death of a father and that of a son. This is achieved by calculating compound interest growth rates – the rates being those that would raise the father's estate size to that of his son over the period of the intergeneration span. The hypothesis proposed is that the criterion for determining whether a man is self-made should be that he achieves a high compound interest growth rate, rather than that he should leave a certain multiple of the estate left by his father.

'Galtonian' Regressions. A third measure of quantifying the importance of inheritance employs the techniques of Galtonian regression analysis to the relationship between the wealth of fathers and sons. This altogether different approach to the question incorporates the familiar law of proportionate effect and is allocated a chapter on its own (Chapter 7). The method involves certain familiar techniques of estimating the association between two variables – fathers' wealth and sons' wealth – through least squares regressions. In addition, an attempt is made to apportion causes of changes in the distribution of personal wealth to the two factors of inheritance and chance.

Tabulated Comparisons
The statistical techniques described in the previous section are used in the following chapters for two main purposes, first to examine trends in the importance of inherited wealth over the period studied (time series), and second to contrast measures of inheritance employed according to various characteristics of different wealth leavers (cross section).[31]

Time Series. Trends in the importance of inheritance are examined by comparing the proportions of wealthy persons who were preceded by wealthy relatives of the same family who left estates of different sizes.[32] Classifications by age are analysed separately in order to examine the extent to which the statistics are distorted e.g. by gifts *inter vivos*. Tabulations are also presented showing the proportions of rich sons who were preceded by fathers leaving more or less than *the minimum wealth needed to qualify for inclusion in the top 10 per cent of wealth holders* at any particular time. Finally, the Galtonian regression techniques are applied exclusively to the time series data, because the numbers involved cannot justify using them in other ways. In the analysis of trends over time, heavy reliance is placed on valuations at constant prices.

Probability Distributions. An alternative way of considering the meaning that can be attached to data of the proportions of rich sons who had been preceded by rich fathers is to attempt to compare them with estimates of the probability that any randomly selected sample of sons for a given year would have been preceded by rich fathers *on the assumption that no association existed* between the wealth of fathers and of sons. Moreover, if such probabilities have changed significantly over the period covered by the study, this could materially affect the interpretation put on the results. For this purpose the estimation of a number of probability distributions of fathers' estates for each of the three samples of top male wealth leavers was necessary.

The probability, for an individual, of having a father leaving an estate of a given size depends on the size distribution of all estates in the year of father's death. For example, if there were 1,000 deaths in total, of which one individual was a millionaire, the chance for any single person of having a millionaire father would be 1 in 1,000 – i.e. the probability would be 0·1 per cent ($P = 0·001$). The probability for a group of individuals whose fathers died over several years depends, therefore, on the size distribution of estates of those dying in all years in which fathers died, *weighted* by the numbers of fathers dying in each year. These are the bases of the probability distributions calculated from IR data for each of the three samples of top wealth leavers of 1956–7, 1965 and 1973. The weights for each year are the actual numbers of fathers in the three samples of sons who died in each year.[33] The results of these calculations are shown in Table 2.7.

Table 2.7   *Probability of Drawing at Random a Father's Estate of a Given Size (Males Only) Per Cent*

	Year of Son's Death		
Size of Father's Estate	1956–7	1965	1973
Over £100,000	0·106	0·128	0·136
50,000	0·256	0·321	0·348
25,000	0·565	0·742	0·830
10,000	1·257	1·904	2·232
5,000	2·303	3·499	4·089
1,000	6·847	10·326	12·318

Sources: Reports of Commissioners of Inland Revenue and Inland Revenue Statistics.
Note: Weighted average numbers of estates per cent of the population dying are shown on this table. Weights are based on the distribution of dates of death of fathers for each of the three sample years.

Table 2.7 shows the probability of drawing at random a person whose father left an estate of more than a given size for each of the years 1956–7, 1965 and 1973. It shows that, for example, for those who died in 1956–7 approximately 1 in every 1,000 (106 in every 100,000) might have expected to have had fathers who left more than £100,000. The table shows more generally that the probability of having been preceded by a wealthy father has tended to rise between the fifties and seventies of this century, though the fall in numbers of rich persons dying in the depression of the 1930s moderated the rise between 1965 and 1973. The figures in Table 2.7 are at current prices. Constant price calculations can be made by taking the price level in 1973 to be roughly double that of 1956–7: for example, comparing an estate of £50,000 in the latter year with one of £100,000 in 1973 – i.e. comparing the probability of 0·256 with one of 0·136. Conclusions based upon constant, rather than current prices tend to show declining, rather than increasing probabilities of drawing a rich father at random. However, the main purpose to which Table 2.7 is put in the analysis in Chapter 3 is to compare the *observed* proportions of sons having wealthy fathers with the numbers *expected* on a hypothesis of no association between the wealth of fathers and sons. Conclusions based upon such comparisons are not affected in any material way by differences between the estimates at constant and current prices.

Cross Section Analysis. Chapter 6 is devoted to analyses of the characteristics of the sample populations which are most frequently associated with self-made and with inherited wealth. The detailed tabulations are determined by those characteristics available for a high enough proportion of the samples to be worthwhile. The principal variable is the occupation of both fathers and sons. The Standard Industrial Classification (SIC) provided the framework.[34] The information leading to the identification of an occupation and the placing of an individual in an SIC category was gleaned from a variety of sources – directories, birth, death and marriage certificates, wills, entries in the Directory of Directors, correspondence with relatives, etc. Inevitably demarcation decisions were not always easy, but after the creation of a 'new' SIC category for those with multiple directorships, where the main interest was not clear, about 90 per cent of the cases were allocated into one of the SIC classes.

Separate analysis was also carried out by age, sex and social status. Age has already been referred to in the previous section as indicating something about the practice of giving *inter vivos*. It is also of interest in another way in throwing light on the life cycle hypothesis.

Sub-Classifications
Analyses were conducted by sex of decedent. Because of the importance of women as wealth holders, a separate chapter is devoted to considerations of the sources of women's wealth, emphasising inheritance from husbands as well as from fathers. By implication this displays information about the pattern and extent of intermarriage among the rich.

Separate classifications were also carried out for persons whose names were listed in the biographical dictionaries such as *Who's Who* and *Debrett's* – here dubbed VIPs.

Finally, in order to put some quantitative order of magnitude on the importance of non-paternal sources of inheritance, analyses were made of family wealth relationships other than between father and son. Tabulations are presented for certain of the most recent samples of top male wealth leavers of the estates of their fathers-in-law, wives, mothers, grandfathers and other relatives. They include also an estimate of the wealth of the 'highest (wealthiest) predecessor'.

The results of the research are presented as follows:

Chapter 3 deals with trends between 1902 and 1973 in the relationship between the wealth of fathers and sons.

Chapter 4 extends the analysis to cover inheritances from relatives other than fathers.

Chapter 5 deals separately with the importance and sources of women's wealth.

Chapter 6 attempts to identify characteristics of wealth holders more commonly associated with inheritors than with the self-made.

Chapter 7 attempts a fresh approach to the analysis of the father–son wealth relationship discussed in Chapter 3 in order that some more general statement may be made about the changing role of inheritance in this country over the last seventy years.

Chapter 8 summarises the conclusions.

NOTES

1   Data used are similar (subject to the qualifications noted in Chapter 1 and the remainder of this chapter) to those used by the Inland Revenue to estimate the distribution of wealth for the living population from that of the decedents for a given year.

2   Alphabetical sampling is assumed to be random (Gray, 1958). There did not appear to be any firm evidence that this is not the case as far as the purposes of this research are concerned. Moreover, the extremely time-consuming fieldwork would have been even more so on any other sampling basis. The full lists of names of men and women in all the samples are available from the authors on request for the cost of photocopying.

3   The numbers of estates lower down the distribution in sample II for 1973 were stratified to include 30 names for each of the following classes – £15,000–£17,499, £17,500–£19,999, £20,000–£29,999, £30,000–£39,999, £40,000–£49,999, £50,000–£59,999, £60,000–£69,999, £70,000–£99,999, £100,000–£149,999, £150,000–£199,999.

4   The sample names in this case were those actually selected by Wedgwood (1929).

5   The date can be approximate only because births are registered by quarters and not by years and also because the reporting is obviously not done by the decedent but by a relative or other person. It is known that the error involved exceeds one year in about 3 per cent of cases. (See the *General Report of the Census of Population of England and Wales*, 1951, Chapter II, 1958.) For the sample of top wealth leavers the error turned out to be rather less; largely one of overestimation of the true age of the deceased. The change in 1970 to requiring date of birth instead of age at death mainly helped because reporters usually seem to get birthday dates right, even if the exact year is wrong; moreover, if the month is correct there is a three-fold reduction in the number of quarterly volumes to be searched.

6   Correspondence was engaged in not only where predecessors' estates were not traced but also in some cases where they had been, in order to check their accuracy.

7   There were, of course, one or two extravagant replies. One widow of a Lt Col, whose title we did not use, wrote 'that if you require urgent information from persons of the upbringing and social status of my husband and his relatives your approach should be more civil'. She had received the same letter as the hundreds of other people who had co-operated. A very diplomatically worded letter was then sent to her without eliciting any response. The father's estate in this case was in fact later traced by examining adjoining graves in the local churchyard. He had been an engineer, who turned out to have left some £12,000 in 1914. Incidentally, no letters were sent to any relatives until at least two years after the death in order to minimise any possible distress.

8   Some gave more information than required. One reported very frankly, for instance, that his client enjoyed the local reputation of being 'something of a Rachmanite'.

9   One example is worth quoting. We met an employee of a spinster, of no apparent occupation, and about whom we were uncertain of the source of her wealth and in particular whether she was perhaps, in one sense, self-made. Her probated estate in 1973 was worth approximately £350,000 and her builder father left about £30,000 in the 1930s. We discovered that she had retained unchanged the identical seventy properties left by her father and the difference in value was entirely accounted for by changing house prices.

10   For the 1902 and 1924–6 samples where we were searching for sons, we obtained actuarial estimates of the number probably still living. These were 0 to 1 and 15 to 20 respectively. We are indebted to Mr S. Haberman, lecturer in Actuarial Science at The City University for these estimates.

11   Such data might become available if proposals such as those of Sandford, Willis and Ironside (1973) for an Accession Tax were ever introduced.

12   Not being able to see the affidavits listing the assets of estates, reliance had to be placed on wills, many of which were highly conditional with complex provisions for shares in family business, pieces of real estate etc. See Horsman (1978).

13   There is a possible small geographical bias regarding Scottish estates. The facts are that all Scottish estates are covered in the Somerset House Calendars, so long as the deceased held some property in England and Wales. This is not quite the same basis as the Inland Revenue use in their statistics for including Scottish estates which is whether they were administered in Scotland or not.

14   The evidence on gifts *inter vivos* is considered in Horsman (1975) and Whalley (1974).

15   A discretionary trust is one where a person puts money or other assets into trust for a number of beneficiaries, but does not specify their shares in it. The trustees are given the discretion to distribute the proceeds of the trust according to their own judgement. In discretionary trusts prior to 1969, no death duty was payable on the death of a beneficiary on his share because it was not regarded as sufficiently definite. (For a *non*-discretionary trust of e.g. £1,000,000 where there were four equal sharing beneficiaries, the estate of each would be valued at £250,000 on the beneficiary's death.)

16   A few unfortunates had trusts drafted so badly that they turned out to be dutiable rather than discretionary.

17   Another reason for differences arises from the fact that the probate valuations entered on the Calendars are those originally made for the purpose of the Inland Revenue affidavit. When any alteration is made the affidavit is resworn, but since 1946 the revised valuations have only rarely been entered in the Calendars. A spot check of original and resworn values for earlier years was made to give some indication of their importance. It must be said that amendments were not particularly common. Where they occurred they rarely affected the value of an estate by more than 2 or 3 percentage points, though in a small number of cases among the largest estates it was more. However, it has almost certainly risen. The Estate Duty Office also kindly produced figures of original and resworn values for seventeen estates actually included in the 1956–7 sample. Since information about named individuals is restricted, the data were supplied for three groups of five or six estates. For those in the two smallest size classes of £50,000 to £100,000 and £100,000 to £200,000, the resworn totals were 3·7 and 3·8 per cent higher. For the largest size group, however (£200,000 and over), the resworn aggregate of the six estates grouped together was 19·6 per cent above the original figure.

18   The deficiency in *capital values* in the top size class was only about 25 per cent in 1974, but this can be accounted for by special circumstances in that this particular year saw the death of Sir John Ellerman, who left over £35,000,000 (probate valuation). This was the largest estate value ever recorded in Britain and exerted a quite disproportionate influence on the statistics.

19   In spite of the availability of net values, gross probate values were used in the study for reasons explained below (see p.26).

20   See Appendix A.

21   This need not hold as an eternal truth, e.g. if tax files were made available to the public

as in certain other countries, or if individuals could be persuaded to supply information about their wealth holdings voluntarily.

22　See Marriott (1967), Appendix I, pp. 267–9. Marriott relied heavily on public records at Companies House; although he stated that the list needed 'heavy qualification', he believed it to give a fair estimate within a margin of 10 per cent either way.

23　When we were fortunate enough to meet Oliver Marriott to discuss the results described above we were impressed at how well informed he appeared to be and also that he did not put forward any reason to doubt the conclusion we had drawn, but rather seemed to accept it as valid.

24　The Returns list landowners by name and by county, giving details of acreage owned and of gross annual values. Wedgwood (1929) capitalised the gross annual values by assuming the following number of years' purchase: 1875, 30 yp; 1885, 23 yp; 1895, 15 yp for rural property and 15 yp throughout for urban realty. He also accepted the corrections to the Returns contained in Bateman (1883). Unfortunately settled land is only included in the probate valuations since 1926.

25　It would, of course, have been possible to estimate the net value of an estate from the duty paid in years before 1934, given the rates of estate duty. However, abatements of duty allowable for certain types of property and non-aggregability accorded others mean that the grossed-up values were not in general significantly more reliable than the gross values of estates themselves.

26　In an interview we conducted the total gifts *inter vivos* we were told had taken place turned out to be almost exactly the same as the difference between the gross and the net of duty value of the estate. This may, of course, have been a coincidence.

27　In point of fact, the matter was thought insufficiently important to exclude the six estates in the results here. They were, however, excluded in the paper by Harbury and Hitchens (1976) to which reference may be made for an assessment of their effect.

28　These adjusted estimates are not included in the analyses of this book because data have now been collected over a much wider period so that the particular comparison between the 1920s and the 1950s is no longer of the same importance (Harbury, 1962).

29　Such a procedure incorporates an adjustment for changes in the total of personal wealth in real terms and its distribution, as well as for changes in the price level.

30　The exact number was not always identifiable from the father's will. But searches in the Births Registers in the GRO provided added confidence in the numbers used.

31　Certain of the results have been published in the *Economic Journal* (Harbury, 1962; Harbury and McMahon, 1973; Harbury and Hitchens, 1976; and Harbury and Hitchens, 1977), and the *Review of Income and Wealth* (Harbury, Hitchens and McMahon, 1977). Readers of these earlier papers may notice that the numbers in some of the tables in Chapters 3–5 below differ marginally from those in the journals. This is because some gaps in the data at the time of publication have been filled by recent research concluded with additional funds. The changes are in fact extremely small quantitatively and in no case make any significant change to the conclusions.

32　Comparisons between proportions were tested by using the t-test, and where significant are marked with asterisks in the tables.

33　For certain years the IR statistics did not provide a distribution by sex of the breakdown of estates and in some years the size classes used did not correspond with others. In these cases graphical interpolation was used to complete the process. We gratefully acknowledge help received from Mr W. Gonzales of the Inland Revenue in this part of the work.

34　The 1958 version of the SIC was adopted because of the large size of the 1956–7 sample. Twenty-five Orders were employed.

3
The Inheritances of Male
Wealth Leavers, 1900–1973

> Riches have wings and sometimes they fly away of
> themselves, sometimes they must be set flying to bring in
> more.
>
> Francis Bacon, *Essay XXXXIV, Of Riches*

This chapter deals with trends in the relationship between fathers' and
sons' wealth since 1900. The analysis is based upon two different *kinds* of
samples. The first examines wealth of the predecessors of three samples
of rich sons dying in 1973, 1965 and 1956–7 (the backward tracing
samples). The second (the forward tracing samples) examines the wealth
of the successors of two samples of rich *fathers* dying in 1902 and
1924–6.[1] The first type of sampling procedure helps answer the kind of
question, 'What proportion of rich individuals are likely to be rich
through substantial inheritances, and what proportion are self-made?'.
The second kind considers the question, 'What proportions of the sons
of rich men managed to increase or dissipate their inheritances?'.

It must be stressed at the outset that this analysis is largely based upon
the values of estates left at death by fathers and sons. Such values are no
better than proxy measures of inheritances. For instance, having a rich
father is likely to be a proxy for having rich relatives. Likewise, a father's
estate is a proxy for the pecuniary transfers made to a son during his
father's lifetime as well as at death. And of course there are the non-
pecuniary advantages that are bestowed upon those born to rich families
such as education, contacts and other associated environmental advantages.[2] In the absence of huge resources it is not possible to trace the
wealth of predecessors along all lines of inheritance, nor to allow for all
gifts *inter vivos*, benefits under trusts, etc., etc. While the data therefore
have inevitable shortcomings, they are in our view capable of throwing
up relevant conclusions. All tables which follow must, however, be
interpreted with these shortcomings in mind.

The arrangement of the chapter is as follows. First the wealth of the
fathers of the three samples of sons dying in 1973, 1965 and 1956–7 is
examined. The father–son wealth relationship is then separately examined for three size classes of sons' wealth – that of 'top' wealth
holders, of 'medium' and of 'small' wealth holders. The proportions of
top wealth holders who may be considered self-made is examined and

trends in the proportions of self-made over time are analysed. This is followed by a discussion of the father–son wealth relationship associated with those in the forward tracing samples and the proportions of sons who accumulated or dissipated their inheritance is examined.

The remainder of the chapter is concerned with the use of alternative methods of analysing the wealth relationship.

THE IMPORTANCE OF FATHERS' WEALTH IN THE BACKWARD TRACING SAMPLES

Table 3.1 shows the relationship between sons' wealth and fathers' wealth in three sampling years – 1956–7, 1965 and 1973. The data are in current prices (i.e. those ruling in the years of death of each father and son). The columns break down the size of the son's estate into wealth groups ranging from £15,000 to £500,000 and over. Each row indicates a sons' wealth interval. The figure in each cell is, therefore, the cumulative percentage of fathers whose estates are greater than a particular size. Starting at the extreme left of the first row which relates to sons leaving £500,000 and over in 1973, it can be seen that 9 per cent were preceded by fathers who left more than £1,000,000; similarly by 14 per cent who left £500,000 or more, by 18 per cent who left £250,000 or more, and so on.

For sons' estates of over £100,000 data are shown on the father–son wealth relationship for each of the three sampling years – 1973, 1965 and 1956–7. Only in 1956–7 and 1973 were samples drawn and a systematic search made for the fathers of sons leaving smaller estates. Data are shown for the wealth of fathers of sons in 1956–7 leaving between £50,000 and £100,000, and in 1973 sons' wealth is further extended downwards to those leaving £15,000 and more.[3]

A more detailed examination of the relationship will be made in the sections which follow. Greater importance will be attached in particular to adjusted data which allow for the different price levels existing at the dates of death of each father and son. However, even in money terms, in spite of the great changes in values that occurred over the period of approximately 100 years from the date of death of the first father to that of the last son, it can be seen from Table 3.1 that the relative importance of fathers' wealth declines as the size of sons' estates fall. If, for example, one arbitrarily examines the proportions of fathers who left more than £50,000 it can be seen that this falls as sons' estate size class diminishes. In 1973, of those sons leaving more than £500,000, 54 per cent were preceded by fathers leaving over £50,000, whereas the proportion is only 2 per cent for sons leaving estates of between £25,000 and £50,000.

Comparisons at Constant Prices
In order that meaningful comparisons may be made between the relationship of fathers' and sons' wealth both for different wealth brackets and between the three sampling years, it is necessary to make allowance for changes that took place in prices over the entire period covering the death of all fathers and sons. This is done in Table 3.2 which

Table 3.1 Estates of Fathers and Sons Dying in 1956–7, 1965 and 1973 (current prices)

Size of Son's Estate	Sample Year	Size of Father's Estate: Cumulative Percentages										Sample Size
		Over £1,000,000	Over £500,000	Over £250,000	Over £100,000	Over £50,000	Over £25,000	Over £10,000	Over £5,000	Over £1,000	All	
£500,000 and over	1973	9	14	18	41	54	64	68	77	82	100	22
	1965	0	11	33	33	56	67	67	67	67	100	9
	1956–7	8	20	28	46	52	68	76	76	80	100	25
£300,000 and under £500,000	1973	0	0	3	21	38	41	55	63	79	100	29
	1965	0	0	25	50	58	75	100	100	100	100	12
	1956–7	2	10	27	41	51	59	63	66	78	100	41
£200,000 and under £300,000	1973	0	2	7	22	30	43	59	72	73	100	56
	1965	0	6	6	22	45	61	61	67	89	100	18
	1956–7	0	3	14	28	47	62	69	70	83	100	71
£100,000 and under £200,000	1973	0	0	2	2	15	22	43	56	72	100	54
	1965	0	0	3	12	28	36	50	62	74	100	99
	1956–7	1	3	9	25	39	55	66	71	82	100	395
£50,000 and under £100,000	1973	0	0	1	3	8	18	31	48	68	100	77
£25,000 and under £100,000	1956–7	0	0	0	9	31	45	56	62	75	100	87
£25,000 and under £50,000	1973	0	0	0	0	2	9	24	42	61	100	59
£15,000 and under £25,000	1973	0	0	0	0	0	2	6	16	37	100	69

Table 3.2 Estates of Fathers and Sons Dying in 1956–7, 1965 and 1973, (constant prices)

Size of Son's Estate	Sample Year	Size of Father's Estate: Cumulative Percentages										Sample Size
		Over £1,000,000	Over £500,000	Over £250,000	Over £100,000	Over £50,000	Over £25,000	Over £10,000	Over £5,000	Over £1,000	All	
£500,000 and over	1973	17	17	50	50	50	50	83	83	83	100	6
	1965	17	17	33	50	50	50	50	50	67	100	6
	1956–7	32	40	40	60	76	76	80	80	84	100	25
£300,000 and under £500,000	1973	29	43	43	72	86	86	86	86	86	100	7
	1965	14	43	57	72	100	100	100	100	100	100	7
	1956–7	22	32	46	56	64	66	68	71	81	100	41
£200,000 and under £300,000	1973	11	21	21	42	58	68	74	84	84	100	19
	1965	0	18	46	73	91	100*	100	100	100	100	11
	1956–7	11	23	35	55	66	69†	73†	82	85	100	71
£100,000 and under £200,000	1973	3	8	16	29	40	51	67	68	76	100	76
	1965	3	7	17	37	46	62	73	77	80	100	70
	1956–7	6	16	30*†	49*	61*†	67*	76	79*	85	100	395
£50,000 and under £100,000	1973	2	2	5	11†	21†	33	51	63	79	100	57
	1965	0	2	13	27	36	42	58	65	80	100	45
	1956–7	0	5	14	37*	47*	57*	68*	73	84	100	87
£25,000 and under £50,000	1973	1	1	3	8	20	31	47	56	69	100	74
£10,000 and under £25,000	1973	0	0	0	1	6	15	36	46	60	100	78
£7,500 and under £10,000	1973	0	0	0	0	0	0	6	17	38	100	47

* Statistically significantly different from the 1973 sample at the 5 per cent level.
† Statistically significantly different from the 1965 sample at the 5 per cent level.

shows the data in Table 3.1 adjusted on the basis of constant 1956–7 prices. The deflator used here is that of the index of retail prices.[4] There are many other possible methods of deflation and some of these will be considered later in this chapter.

The effect of deflating sons' estates at constant prices can be seen in the way in which sons dying in 1973 and 1965 are reclassified into lower estate size intervals in accordance with the lower price level of 1956–7. The effect of inflating fathers' estates increases their size in constant prices. From Table 3.2 the percentages of sons whose fathers left varying amounts can now be compared within each year and between each sampling year. Hence if sons whose estates fell in the size class over £500,000 are examined (i.e. those in the top left-hand corner of the table) it can be seen that 32 per cent in 1956–7 were preceded by fathers leaving more than £1,000,000, whereas in both 1965 and 1973 the proportions were 17 per cent. Furthermore, the importance of fathers' wealth in most cases tends to decline as sons' estate size diminishes in each sample year, as was noted from Table 3.1. The rate of decline, however, is not the same for each sampling year. This may be due to two influences. The first is that of sampling error and it can be seen that the number of observations, particularly in the highest sons' size classes and in the last two sample years, is small. However, statistical tests of those proportions of fathers leaving estates of different sizes were undertaken, and those which are significantly different between sampling years are marked and these will be discussed below.[5]

The second influence which makes difficult a comparison of the importance of fathers' wealth for sons leaving very large estates (and especially those of above £100,000) is that there is reason to suspect that the distribution is likely to be truncated at the upper end as a result of the use of tax avoidance practices. This means that one should be cautious about differentiating between two men who died in the postwar period whose estates were valued for probate say at £200,000 and £400,000 because their 'true' wealth might be very similar. Some light was thrown on this in Chapter 2, Table 2.5, where a comparison of the estates left at death by a number of believed millionaires is shown. The table tended to confirm the view that the very wealthy are likely to leave at least £100,000 at probate but their actual wealth in some cases may have been much greater than this.

Not only does Table 3.2 show that the proportions of all fathers leaving various amounts tends to diminish as sons' estate size class falls, but it also gives a first look at the fact that a number of sons were likely to have been dissipators. Thus, if attention is drawn to sons in the wealth size class £25,000 to £50,000 it can be seen that 3 per cent were preceded by fathers leaving more than £250,000. Discussion of the relative importance of accumulation and dissipation among the wealthy is better examined with sample data of the second kind (that of forward tracing where successors' wealth is traced), but some indication of this is given in Table 3.2 by examining the proportions of fathers leaving estates greater than that of their sons.

The data presented in Table 3.2 are next analysed for different wealth size classes of sons' estates – those of 'top', 'medium' and 'small' wealth leavers. The nomenclature may be misleading. Even the 'small' wealth leavers are well within the top 10 per cent of wealthy individuals. Similarly 'medium' wealth leavers fall within that of the top 1 per cent and 'top' wealth leavers are among the top 0·1 per cent of the distribution.[6]

Although the figures in the tables so far represent a continuous series of sons' wealth, it is useful to be able to distinguish between those wealth holders who may be described as very wealthy and further to examine the number who are substantial inheritors or self-made men. Interpretation of the data in the other two categories of sons' wealth will be concerned rather more with patterns of inheritance and changes over time.

TOP WEALTH LEAVERS

Table 3.3 shows the father–son wealth relationship for all sons leaving over £100,000. The top four sons' wealth intervals in Table 3.2 have been collapsed into one row because of the suspected truncation at the top end of the distribution. (Although there is a perceptibly rising trend in the importance of fathers' wealth in the higher sons' wealth classes interpretation of these is blurred because of truncation.) The table throws light on, first, the proportion of top wealth leavers who may be identified as self-made, and second, the trend in the importance of fathers' wealth over time.

The discussion which follows will involve the setting out of necessarily arbitrary criteria to try and answer this first question. It is followed by certain tests and methods of analysis. The question of changing trends in the importance of fathers' wealth among top wealth leavers is also subject to qualifications particularly of the kind which may be reflected in the quality of the data. A quite different method of deciding these questions is contained in Chapter 7.

Table 3.3 shows the relationship between top wealth leavers and the wealth of their fathers for each of the three sampling years. It can be seen for example that for all sons leaving more than £100,000, 36 per cent were preceded by fathers leaving wealth above this level in the 1973 sample and 45 and 51 per cent in the 1965 and 1956–7 samples. Over 70 per cent of fathers left estates in excess of £10,000 (in all samples).

Inheritors versus Self-made
No single definition of 'having a rich father' can, of course, be unambiguously determined. Two approaches can be considered initially. The first is that having a rich father requires that a father should leave as much as his son. Referring back to the first row of Table 3.2 it can be seen that in 1973 17 per cent of sons leaving more than £500,000 had fathers leaving as much or more than this level of wealth. The remaining 83 per cent have accumulated above the size of their fathers'

Table 3.3 *Estates of Fathers of Top Male Wealth Leavers of 1956–7, 1965 and 1973 (constant prices)*

Size of Son's Estate	Sample Year	Size of Father's Estate: Cumulative percentages										Sample Size
		Over £1,000,000	Over £500,000	Over £250,000	Over £100,000	Over £50,000	Over £25,000	Over £10,000	Over £5,000	Over £1,000	All	
All over £100,000	1973	7	13	21	36	47	58	71	74	79	100	108
	1965	4	12	24	45	55	68	77	80	83	100	94
	1956–7	9	19	33*	51*	63*	68*	75	78	85	100	532

* Statistically significantly different from the 1973 sample at the 5 per cent level.

Table 3.4 *Estates of Fathers of Medium Wealth Leavers of 1956–7, 1965 and 1973 (constant prices)*

Size of Son's Estate	Sample Year	Size of Father's Estate: Cumulative percentages										Sample Size
		Over £1,000,000	Over £500,000	Over £250,000	Over £100,000	Over £50,000	Over £25,000	Over £10,000	Over £5,000	Over £1,000	All	
£50,000 and under £100,000	1973	2	2	5	11†	21†	33	51	63	79	100	57
	1965**	0	2	13	27	36	42	58	65	80	100	45
	1956–7	0	5	14	37*	47*	57*	68*	73	84	100	87

** Between £80,000 and £100,000 only.
* Statistically significantly different from the 1973 sample at the 5 per cent level.
† Statistically significantly different from the 1965 sample at the 5 per cent level.

estate and, therefore, at one extreme one might use the notion of accumulation to distinguish those who are in some sense self-made. This notion of accumulation will be returned to in a later section.

An alternative depends on being able to state with some degree of confidence a money value of wealth which would be taken to describe a lower limit to those bracketed as 'rich'. This approach provides a useful first approximation.

It may be suggested in this light that sums of £50,000, £25,000 and even £10,000 for fathers' wealth (in constant prices) might be taken as lines of demarcation between the inheritors and the self-made. Each would still place fathers well within the top 10 per cent of wealth holders. At a cut-off point of £50,000, 47 per cent, 55 per cent and 63 per cent of the 1973, 1965 and 1956–7 samples would be classed as substantial inheritors. Alternatively a level of fathers' wealth above £25,000 would imply that 58 per cent of the 1973 sample and 68 per cent of the 1965 and 1956–7 samples are substantial inheritors. On this last definition just over 40 per cent of top male wealth leavers in 1973 are self-made and nearly one-third of the 1965 and 1956–7 samples. The proportion naturally depends upon which watershed is chosen.

MEDIUM WEALTH LEAVERS

Samples of estates were drawn for size classes below the £100,000 top wealth limit for both the years 1956–7 and 1973. The 1973 sample includes estates of above £15,000 and that of 1956–7 of above £50,000. This section is concerned with fathers in a middle range here termed 'medium' wealth leavers. It is possible to compare the substantial wealth of sons in the £50,000 to £100,000 bracket with that of their fathers in a similar way to that shown above in Table 3.3.

Before attention is drawn to the results in Table 3.4 it should be mentioned that the search for sons leaving £50,000 and over in 1965 was a non-systematic one. The estates in the bracket £50,000 to £100,000 in the table for that year appear solely as a result of the process of reducing sons' estates of £100,000 and over to constant prices. £100,000 in 1965 is equivalent to approximately £80,000 in 1956–7 prices and the figures presented relate to values above this level and are therefore not strictly comparable with those for 1956–7 and 1973. At the level of sons' wealth of £50,000 to £100,000 the relative importance of inheritance as measured here in comparison with that of top wealth holders (shown in Table 3.3 above) is smaller. For example, 51 per cent of fathers left £10,000 or over (in the 1973 sample), whereas among top wealth leavers 71 per cent of fathers left more than this level of wealth. Indeed at all levels of fathers' wealth above £5,000 in each of the three samples inheritance is relatively less important among sons classified as 'medium' wealth holders.

SMALLER ESTATES

Table 3.5 also abstracts from Table 3.2 for separate examination data on the father–son wealth relationship for sons dying in 1973 in the lowest of the three wealth categories employed here – those leaving less than £50,000. It should be emphasised, however, that estates dubbed here 'smaller' nevertheless include wealth leavers well within the top 10 per cent of wealth holders in 1973. The proportions in each row show the diminishing importance of fathers' wealth as sons' wealth decreases. In the sons' smallest wealth category, as might be expected, fathers' wealth is relatively unimportant and for example 6 per cent were preceded by fathers leaving more than £10,000. Above the smallest size class of sons' wealth it can be seen from Table 3.5 that the importance of fathers' wealth rises steeply – in the sons' wealth intervals of £10,000 to £25,000 and £25,000 to £50,000 the proportions of sons preceded by fathers leaving more than, for example, £10,000 rises sharply to 36 and 47 per cent, and this trend of rising importance of fathers' wealth can be seen for other estate intervals in the table.

Figure 3.1 summarises the relationship between fathers' and sons' wealth for the three categories of 'top', 'medium' and 'smaller' estates. For this purpose the data over the period have been pooled for each category of wealth leaver. The horizontal axis of the figure represents the logarithm of fathers' wealth and the vertical axis measures the cumulative percentages of fathers leaving estates in excess of varying amounts. The lines then show for each of the three categories of wealth leavers the cumulative percentages of fathers leaving estates of varying size. The nature of the graph is that the further away from the origin to the north-east the greater is the importance of inheritance. It is clearly illustrated in the figure that fathers' wealth becomes increasingly important as the sons' wealth category rises. Indeed if the data as a whole are examined in Table 3.2, it can be seen that this close relationship exists between the wealth of fathers and sons throughout the distribution.

An important issue which will concern us later arises from the nature of the changing degree of the relationship between sons' and fathers' wealth as sons' wealth interval rises. Whether the expected truncation at the top end of the distribution referred to above would suggest that the statistical relationship between fathers' and sons' wealth would be more reliably estimated from the data for medium and small wealth leavers will be examined in Chapter 7.

PROBABILITIES OF DYING RICH

It is important to compare the data on the father–son wealth relationship shown in all the tables above with one which indicates the chances of having a father leaving an estate of various sizes if there were *no* relationship between a son's wealth and that of his father. This is done in Table 3.6 which examines the probability of selecting by chance a father's estate of any particular size for each of the three sample years.[7]

Table 3.6 shows, for example, that the chance of drawing at random an estate of over £100,000 was 0·11 per cent in 1956–7 and 0·13 and 0·14

Table 3.5 *Estates of Fathers of Small Wealth Leavers of 1973 (constant prices)*

Size of Son's Estate	Sample	Size of Father's Estates: Cumulative Percentages									All	Sample Size
		Over £1,000,000	Over £500,000	Over £250,000	Over £100,000	Over £50,000	Over £25,000	Over £10,000	Over £5,000	Over £1,000		
£25,000 and under £50,000	1973	1	1	3	8	20	31	47	56	69	100	74
£10,000 and under £25,000	1973	0	0	0	1	6	15	36	46	60	100	78
£7,500 and under £10,000	1973	0	0	0	0	0	0	6	17	38	100	47

Figure 3.1   *Estates of fathers of wealth leavers, by size class of sons' estates, 1956–7, 1965 and 1973 (pooled)*
(Percentages of fathers leaving estates in excess of different values)

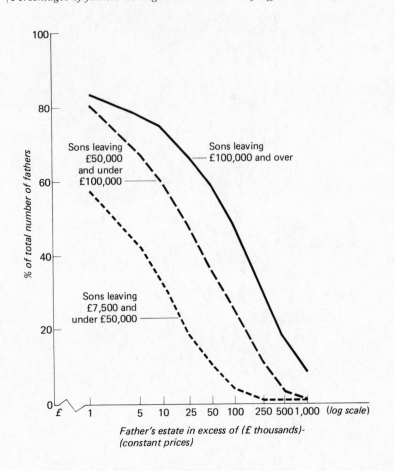

per cent in 1965 and 1973. Similarly the chance of drawing an estate of over £1,000 was 6·85 per cent in 1956–7 and 10·33 and 12·32 per cent in the latter two sampling years.

If these probabilities are now compared with the data in Table 3.1 which gives the observed relationship between fathers' and sons' wealth in current prices, it can be seen that for all levels of sons' wealth the proportion of fathers leaving estates of varying size greatly exceeds that of a random relationship. For example, 41 per cent of fathers whose sons left over £500,000 left more than £100,000 in 1973. On the basis of chance just 0·14 per cent of fathers would be expected to leave estates above this level of wealth. It must be concluded therefore that fathers' wealth is an important correlate of sons' wealth.

Table 3.6 *Probability of Drawing at Random a Father's Estate of a
Given Size (Males only) Per Cent (current prices)*

	Year of Son's Death		
Size of Estate	1956–7	1965	1973
Over £100,000	0·106	0·128	0·136
50,000	0·256	0·321	0·348
25,000	0·565	0·742	0·830
10,000	1·257	1·904	2·232
5,000	2·303	3·499	4·089
1,000	6·847	10·326	12·318

Source: Reports of Commissioners of Inland Revenue and Inland Revenue Statistics.
Notes: (a) Weighted average numbers of estates per cent of the population dying are
shown in this table. Weights are based on the distribution of dates of death of fathers for
each of the three sample years.
   (b) See pp.32–4 above for full explanation of assumptions on which based.

TRENDS OVER TIME

This section is concerned with trends in the importance of fathers'
wealth over time. The following analyses are confined to the data on the
'top' wealth leavers and 'medium' wealth leavers.

*Top Male Wealth Leavers: Trends in the Importance of Fathers'
Wealth*

Table 3.3 showed that there had been a fairly steady decline in the
proportions of rich sons being preceded by rich fathers between the
sample years of the 1950s and 1970s. This is true at virtually all levels of
wealth. Indeed the decline became statistically significant between
1956–7 and 1973 in four fathers' wealth intervals.[8]

The relationships between fathers' and sons' wealth for top wealth
leavers is also depicted in Figure 3.2. The graph measures fathers' estates
along the horizontal axis (in logarithms) while the vertical axis measures
the cumulative percentages of all top wealth leavers who were preceded
by fathers leaving estates of varying size. The closer the curves are to the
vertical axis the less the importance of inheritance and the higher the
proportion of self-made men. It can be seen that the general relationship
is of a movement towards the origin between 1956–7 and 1973, though
the curves do intersect both at the top end of the wealth scale (between
1973 and 1965) and at the lower end of the scale (in the cases of the
1956–7 and 1965 samples).

Before proceeding with the analysis it may be worthwhile pausing to
consider possible reasons for the apparent increase in the proportions of
self-made men among those dying since the Second World War. The
potential explanations are many. In so far as very heavy tax rates on
large estates led to increasing use of estate duty avoidance practices
including, for example, gifts *inter vivos*, this would tend to make the
decline (at least partly) illusory. The effect would be seen in a reduction

Figure 3.2   *Estates of the fathers of the top wealth leavers of 1956–7, 1965 and 1973*
(Percentages of fathers leaving estates in excess of different values)

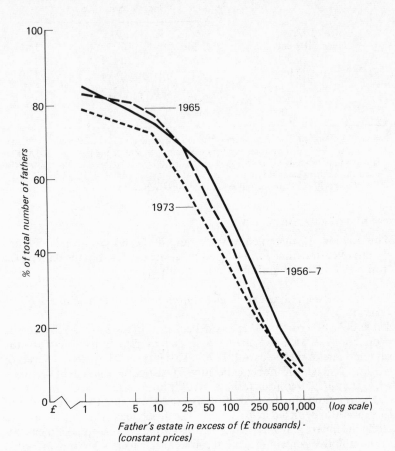

of the size of a father's estate at the time of probate in comparison with the earlier sample years.

Furthermore the tables show only the relationship between estates of a single son and the whole of his father's estate. It does not allow for division of estates among children. Hence the decline in family size that has occurred since the nineteenth century may suggest that the sons of 1973 inherited a larger share of their fathers' estate than did those individuals in the 1956–7 sample. The effect this has on the comparison of individual father's estate size classes between the periods cannot be determined without data on family size over the period covered by the three sample years.

The two issues of an increase in estate duty avoidance and a decrease in family size affect the data in opposite directions. The former tends to reduce the probate value at death of a father's estate whereas the latter tends to increase a son's share over the period.

On the other hand there are real factors which may account for the decline in the importance of inheritance over the period. Detailed examination of such factors is relegated to Chapter 7 where the separate issue of the relative importance of inheritance and self-made factors in determining the changing size distribution of wealth is discussed in greater detail.

Whatever the full explanation for the decline in the importance of inheritance shown in Table 3.3 it is important to restate that fathers' wealth remains a major correlate of large personal fortunes. For example, if one takes £25,000 in real terms, as a minimum definition of being wealthy, then there has been a statistically significant decline (some 10 percentage points) in the proportions of top wealth leavers in 1973 who were preceded by fathers who died rich compared with the earlier decades. None the less, the results show that 58 per cent of the fathers of the wealthy left more than this amount, and this figure may be compared with that of random association (Table 3.6) of less than one-half a per cent.[9]

Medium Wealth Leavers
The trend in the importance of fathers' wealth shows a similar decline among 'medium' wealth leavers which can be seen from Table 3.4, where the decline in proportions of sons preceded by fathers leaving varying amounts is statistically significantly different in a number of cells both between 1973 and 1965, and between 1973 and 1956–7.

COMPARISONS WITH THE 1920s

Examination of the trends in the father–son wealth relationship so far have been restricted to the period 1956–7 to 1973, but a similar analysis was undertaken by Wedgwood in the 1920s and it is from his study that much of the present work springs.

Wedgwood employed somewhat different methods both of sampling and of presenting his data on the father–son relationship. The differences were important enough for a number of adjustments to be made in order to render them more comparable with data for recent years. The methods used are described in Harbury (1962) and the results suggest that there is little difference between the generations of the 1920s and that of the 1950s in the proportions of sons in both the classes of 'top' and 'medium' wealth leavers who were preceded by fathers with various amounts of wealth.

The trend, therefore, has been stable to the 1950s showing an observable decline in 1965 and a statistically significant decline for the first time this century in the 1973 sample.

ACCUMULATORS AND DISSIPATORS OF WEALTH

So far the father–son wealth relationship has been examined for three samples of sons leaving estates of various sizes between 1956–7 and 1973. The way in which the samples were drawn cannot throw direct light on such questions as 'what percentage of rich men's sons dissipated their wealth?' because each father is matched with only one son who is, by definition, rich. For this additional data are needed. Two samples were therefore drawn of rich fathers dying in 1902 and 1924–6 and the wealth left by their sons traced. This procedure allows for a comparison of the wealth of several sons of each rich father for both samples. The method also enables one particular obstacle encountered in the earlier analysis to be overcome. It was possible to obtain an estimate of each son's probable inheritance by dividing each father's estate by the number of his sons. In the earlier samples described above, data on the number of sons were not obtained and it was not therefore possible to examine the father–son wealth relationship on this basis.

FORWARD TRACING SAMPLES

This section examines the two 'forward tracing' samples of 1902 and 1924–6 where the wealth of successors were traced. The samples include rich fathers leaving over £100,000 and £200,000 in the two sampling years respectively. The wealth left by all sons in the 1902 sample were traced, but a number of sons in the 1924–6 sample are still living.[10]

The Results

Table 3.7 shows the relationship between each son's 'inheritance' (defined here as father's estate divided by the number of his sons) and the size of his own estate left at death for both samples.[11] Table 3.7(a) refers to the sample of fathers dying in 1902 and 3.7(b) to those of 1924–6. The column shows the size of the sons' inheritances and the rows show the cumulative percentages of sons leaving estates in excess of different amounts at constant prices. For example, Table 3.7(a) shows that in the 1902 sample of rich fathers, those sons whose share of a father's estate was estimated to be over £250,000, themselves left estates of more than this level of wealth in 35 per cent of cases, while 57 per cent of such sons left estates of above £100,000. The general trend portrayed in the table is of diminishing size of sons' estates being associated with declining inheritance. A similar conclusion was earlier drawn from Table 3.2.

Table 3.7(b) deals with sons in the 1924–6 sample and tells much the same story. If, for example, one examines sons leaving over £100,000, it can be seen that those with an 'inheritance' share of more than £250,000 left themselves more than £100,000 in 50 per cent of cases, whereas 15 per cent left more than this amount in the inheritance size class of between £50,000 and £100,000.

Table 3.7(a) can also be read to throw light on the prevalence of accumulators and dissipators. Defining accumulation and dissipation in terms of the percentage of sons who left more than or less than their inheritance, it can be seen that in the 1902 sample 35 per cent of sons left as much or more than the £250,000 left by their fathers and in the 1924–6

Table 3.7 *Estates of Sons and Fathers dying in 1902 and 1924–6 (constant prices)*
Cumulative Percentages

3.7(a) Fathers dying in 1902

Son's 'Inheritance'	Son's Estate Size						
	Over £250,000	Over £100,000	Over £50,000	Over £25,000	All	Sample Size
Over £250,000	35	57	68	88	100	101
£100,000 and under £250,000	12	26	52	64	100	50
£50,000 and under £100,000	5	32	42	58	100	19
All over £50,000	25	45	61	78	100	170

3.7(b) Fathers dying in 1924–6

Son's 'Inheritance'	Son's Estate Size						
	Over £250,000	Over £100,000	Over £50,000	Over £25,000	All	Sample Size
Over £250,000	32	50	74	85	100	34
£100,000 and under £250,000	17	45	55	69	100	29
£50,000 and under £100,000	0	15	54	77	100	13
All over £50,000	21	42	63	78	100	76

Note: Son's inheritance is defined as father's estate divided by the number of sons. None of the observations between the two samples is statistically significantly different.

sample 32 per cent did so. Lower down the scale at a level of sons' inheritance of between £50,000 and £100,000 the proportions were 42 and 54 per cent respectively. Obversely, therefore, there is a tendency for approximately more than 50 per cent of the sons of rich fathers to dissipate their wealth in each individual 'inheritance' wealth interval.

The results are also shown graphically in Figure 3.3, where the horizontal axis measures the size of sons' estates and the vertical axis the cumulative percentages of sons leaving estates of varying sizes. The graph is based on the total of all sons in each of the samples whose inheritance share exceeds £50,000. It shows a remarkably close and similar association between sons' inheritance and sons' wealth for the two samples. If it is regarded as legitimate to pool the data in the 1902 and 1924–6 samples (because of the close relationship which exists between the results shown in the table) the numbers become large enough to reach more substantial conclusions. When the data are pooled it can be shown from Table 3.7 that 66 per cent of the combined samples dissipated their fortunes while 34 per cent of sons left estates equivalent to or more than their inheritance.

SUMMARY

Two analyses have been undertaken so far in this chapter. The sources of wealth of three samples of wealth leavers have been compared, and the varying propensities to accumulate and dissipate fortunes have been analysed. The remainder of the chapter is concerned with extending and improving the analysis by the use of certain alternative techniques. Different ways of comparing the father–son wealth relationship are presented and the question of the sensitivity of the results to the use of different price indices to deflate fathers' estates is examined.

ALTERNATIVE METHODS: INHERITANCE VERSUS SELF-MADE

The alternative techniques of analysis presented below are mainly concerned with throwing additional light on the question of the proportions of top wealth leavers who might be described as self-made, although some additional data are given, e.g. on the varying rates of accumulation.

Two alternative methods are used. The first is concerned with the *relative* position of fathers in the wealth distribution at their date of death. The second analyses rates of wealth accumulation over the period between dates of death of fathers and sons.

The Relative Wealth of Fathers and Sons

Fathers' and sons' wealth have so far been compared in both current and constant prices. A rather different way of adjusting wealth at various times for changes in the value of money is to relate the wealth of each father to the distribution of wealth existing in the year of his death. Such a method has the advantage of allowing for changes in the general level of prices and in the growth and distribution of wealth over time.

Figure 3.3   *Estates of the sons of the top male wealth leavers of 1902 and 1924–6*
(sons' inheritance in excess of £50,000)
(Percentages of sons leaving estates in excess of different values)

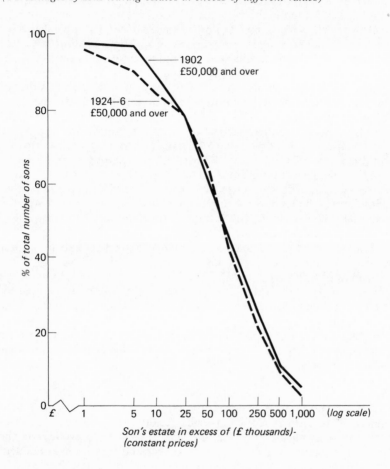

A simple example will illustrate this way of comparing estates. First a measure of wealth distribution is chosen. That used here is the minimum wealth required to place an individual in the top 10 per cent of wealth holders. Suppose, then, two fathers die, each leaving £50,000, but the first in 1900 and the other in 1930. The estates are then related to the position each holds *vis-à-vis* the wealth of the top 10 per cent in each year.[12] In fact, the minimum wealth holding for an individual to be in the top 10 per cent of wealth holders in 1900 was estimated to be approximately £330 and in 1930 £830.[13] Both fathers leave £50,000, but the first by this method of comparing estates is placed higher in the distribution because his estate is a greater multiple of the minimum wealth of £330 than is the case of the father dying in 1930. Hence the first father's estate is 150 times this minimum level of wealth in 1900 while the second is 60 times the minimum in 1930.

Table 3.8 shows the relationship between fathers' and sons' wealth on this basis of estimation for the three 'backward tracing' samples of top male wealth leavers whose fathers died since 1900.[14] The table shows for each of the three samples the various proportions of sons who had fathers with different multiples of the minimum wealth of the top 10 per cent in their year of death. If, for example, the results for 1956–7 are examined, 21 per cent of fathers' estates were at least 250 times that of the minimum wealth of the top 10 per cent of wealth holders in their day. Reading across the row, 87 per cent had a multiple of unity or higher, i.e. were preceded by fathers who were within the top 10 per cent of the wealth distribution at their date of death. The comparable proportions for 1965 and 1973 are 91 and 82 per cent respectively.

The table shows that the relative wealth of fathers of these top wealth leavers was considerable. Over one-third of the 1973 sample and a half of the sons in the 1965 and 1956–7 samples had fathers whose wealth was minimally 50 times that of the minimum wealth of the top 10 per cent of wealth holders at their date of death.

The figures in the table show, on the whole, a trend of relatively poorer fathers of top male wealth leavers between 1956–7 and 1973 for multiples of fathers' estates of 25 and above. For lower multiples, the fathers of the 1973 sample remain relatively poorer than those of 1956–7, though those of 1965 are the relatively richer. The figures in the table tend to confirm the general nature of the results presented earlier, showing a declining proportion of rich fathers of top male wealth leavers between 1956–7 and 1973 with a number of differences in proportions which are statistically significant.

Inheritors versus Self-made and the Relative Wealth of Fathers
Table 3.8 can be used to assess the relative importance of sons with inherited as distinct from self-made wealth. In the former analysis different watersheds based on the size of a father's estate was the suggested approach. Table 3.8 on the other hand permits an assessment of the proportions of those rich sons who might be described as self-made using criteria based on relative wealth.

In order to achieve this it is important in the first place to attach meaning to the different multiples of the minimum wealth of the top 10 per cent. Clearly from the way in which the table has been constructed all those fathers with a multiple of 1 or higher are within the top 10 per cent of wealth holders at their date of death. It is now possible to use a watershed dividing inheritors from self-made using alternative, albeit arbitrary, boundaries. For example, it might be decided to call all whose fathers were in the top 10 per cent of the wealth distribution, inheritors, leaving the remainder to be described as self-made. Alternatively one might elect to include in the former category only those whose fathers held 5, 10 or any multiple of the minimum wealth of the top 10 per cent of the distribution.[15]

Table 3.8 Relative Wealth of Top Male Wealth Leavers, 1956–7, 1965 and 1973

| | Father's estate as a multiple of the minimum wealth of the top 10 per cent at his date of death (cumulative percentages) | | | | | | | | | | |
| | Multiples equal to and above | | | | | | | | | | |
Sample Year	250	100	50	25	15	10	5	3	1	Less than 1	Sample Size
1973	11	30	38	48	60	70	77	79	82	100	97
1965	14	34	52	60	74	75	82	84	91	100	77
1956–7	21*	42*	56*	66*	71*	74	80	81	87	100	431

Note: Son's estates include all top male wealth leavers leaving more than £100,000 in 1956–7 prices.
* Statistically significantly different from the 1973 sample.

If the watershed of the minimum point of entry into the top 10 per cent of the wealth distribution is taken as a means of distinguishing between inheritors and the self-made, then 13, 9 and 18 per cent of those sons in the three samples 1956–7, 1965 and 1973 were self-made. Using multiples of the top 10 per cent of (times) 5 and (times) 10, the proportions become 20, 18 and 23 per cent if the former multiple is used, and 26, 25 and 30 per cent if the latter multiple is taken.

Later in this chapter the results will be further compared with those obtained earlier and later using different criteria.

Compound Interest Growth Rates
In this section a further method of comparing fathers' and sons' estates is considered in order to throw light yet again on the issue of the proportions of sons who should be considered as inheritors or self-made. The principle behind the method involves introducing the time between the dates of death of fathers and sons into the comparison of their estates.

The technique requires the calculation of compound interest growth rates (the rate being that sufficient to raise a father's estate to the size of that of his son over the period of the intergeneration span). The use of this measure for examining the father–son wealth relationship focuses attention on sons who achieve high or low rates of growth, irrespective of the size of a father's estate. The difference involved in using growth rates rather than comparisons of the values of fathers' and sons' estates can be appreciated with the following example. Suppose there are two men who die in the same year, each leaving £100,000 and each being preceded by a father leaving £50,000. Suppose also that one father died twenty and the other two years before his son. On the basis of the criterion used earlier – that men whose fathers left £25,000 or more were inheritors – both sons in this example would be so classed. The growth rate criterion, however, would classify only the first son as an inheritor. Recognising the greater rate of accumulation over two years which the second son achieved, it would classify him among the self-made.

It was thought that the use of growth rates in the analysis might be particularly valuable because the intergeneration span varied a great deal between sons, and this is shown in Table 3.9. The median intergeneration span was approximately forty years but the spread is very wide between zero to over eighty years.[16]

Growth rates were calculated for each sample following the standard formula:

$$P = pa^t$$

where P is the son's estate
         p is the father's estate
         t is the period of the intergeneration span in years
and a is the compound interest growth rate.

In the following analysis the hypothesis is put forward that the decision

Table 3.9   *Intergeneration Spans of Top Male Wealth Leavers*

Years elapsing between date of death of father and that of son	1973 %	per cent of total Sample Year 1965 %	1956–7 %
0–10	2	2	3
11–20	12	11	8
21–30	18	20	17
31–40	18	22	23
41–50	25	18	25
51–60	12	10	13
61–70	9	8	8
71–80	3	7	3
81–90	1	2	1
	100	100	101*

* Percentages are of the total number of individuals in each sample. They do not add up to 100 in every case because of rounding.

to call a rich man self-made depends on the rate of accumulation between the date of his father's and his own death – as measured by the rate of growth of their respective estates. The analysis is sensitive therefore not only to the size of a father's and son's estate but also to the intergeneration span. The employment of the measure of growth rates is naturally imperfect. This is partly because accumulation does not normally occur evenly over a man's lifetime or after his father's death, but is more likely to be concentrated in certain years when he is most productively active. Thus those sons with very long intergeneration spans are not strictly comparable with those with relatively short ones because of the greater probability that the former covered both a period of high growth rates achieved during working lives followed by wealth dissipation in later life according to a simple life-cycle hypothesis.[17]

Rates of Accumulation of Top Male Wealth Leavers of 1956–7, 1965 and 1973

Table 3.10 sets out the pattern of growth rates for each of the three sample years. It can be seen, for example, that 10 per cent of sons' estates in the 1956–7 sample achieved rates of growth of at least 20 per cent per annum, compared with 9 and 18 per cent of sons in the 1965 and 1973 samples respectively. The rates of growth are calculated in constant prices and therefore approximate real rates of return.

The table shows a general tendency for the proportions of sons achieving given growth rates to rise between 1956–7 and 1973. This result may be compared with that drawn from Table 3.3 which is based simply on the size of fathers' estates. Both show a remarkably similar trend. As with the other techniques previously employed in this chapter, the same question arises of the most appropriate bench-mark, here a

Table 3.10 *Compound Interest Growth Rates Between Fathers' and Sons' Estates, Top Wealth Leavers of 1956–7, 1965 and 1973 (constant prices)*

| | | | | | | *Cumulative Percentages* | | | | | | | | |
| | | | | | | *Growth rate equal to or greater than %* | | | | | | | | |
Sample Year	20	15	10	9	8	7	6	5	4	3	2	1	Less than 1	Sample Size
1973	18	22	28	31	33	36	39	45	47	54	63	68	100	108
1965	9	10*	18	21	26	28	30	37	38	46	53	61	100	94
1956–7	10*	15	20	21*	24	26*	29*	31*	36*	39*	43*	52*	100	532

* Statistically significantly different from the 1973 sample at the 5 per cent level.

growth rate, to divide the self-made from inheritors. This is again to some extent an arbitrary decision. The answer might however be thought to be related to the real rate of return at which the average son might have been expected to accumulate from his inheritance without any particular good luck or entrepreneurial skills. To determine such a rate, one needs to know not only the exact length of the intergeneration span but also the portfolio of assets inherited by each son. One method might then be to take the portfolio of assets inherited by a son, assume that he maintained that portfolio over the intergeneration span and ploughed back the income generated from his holding; this would yield a capital sum at his date of death and accordingly a rate of return over the intergeneration span.

In the absence of information on asset portfolios and therefore the appropriate rate for each son, one has to deal with aggregates. For them there fortunately exists a series of real rates of return on equities and fixed interest securities, published by Merrett and Sykes (1966), for the period 1919–66 which can provide the needed bench-mark. Merrett and Sykes' series show that a single lump sum would have grown before tax at compound rates of 8 per cent for equities and 0·0 per cent for fixed interest securities over the span of 47 years, taking capital growth and the stream of dividends into account and making an allowance at the standard rate for tax on dividends. If one then applies this 8 per cent as a watershed, for example, to the set of 1973 sons it indicates that about one-third who achieved a greater rate of growth should be classed as self-made. On the other hand a portfolio of 50 per cent equities and 50 per cent fixed interest securities would yield a real rate of return of 6 per cent – suggesting for 1973 that 39 per cent of sons should be considered self-made. Indeed, given the stringent requirements applied to the series it does not seem unreasonable to adopt 6 per cent as an upper limit. At this percentage level the table shows that the proportions of self-made in each of the three sampling periods are 29 per cent in 1956–7, 30 per cent in 1965 and 39 per cent in 1973, showing a fairly clear upward trend. Alternatively, if a real rate of return of 4 per cent is used the trend remains, with 36, 38 and 47 per cent of self-made sons.

It is of some interest to compare the proportions of self-made men thrown up by the growth rate method with the proportions obtained using the alternative techniques used earlier. Table 3.11 is a first step in this process. It provides a comparison of growth rates achieved by sons, broken down by the size of fathers' estates. The columns measure fathers' estate size while each row shows the (cumulative) percentages of sons achieving various growth rates. If a watershed of £25,000 is taken to discriminate between sons with rich fathers and the self-made, then it can be seen that the growth rate criterion includes cases of estates achieving rates of growth in excess of 6 per cent in fathers' estate size classes above this level of wealth. Hence if father's wealth interval of £25,000 to £50,000 is examined, 27 per cent of the 1973 sample, 8 per cent of the 1965 sample and 25 per cent of the 1956–7 sample whose fathers left this level of wealth would now be considered self-made. Similar

Table 3.11 Compound Interest Growth Rates Between Fathers' and Sons' Estates, Top Wealth Leavers of 1956–7, 1965 and 1973 (constant prices)

Father's Estate Size	Sample	Cumulative Percentages — Growth rates equal to or greater than %												Less than 1	Sample Size
		20	15	10	9	8	7	6	5	4	3	2	1		
£250,000 and over	1973	0	0	0	0	0	0	0	0	0	5	5	5	100	23
	1965	0	0	0	0	0	0	0	0	0	0	0	0	100	23
	1956–7	0	0	0	0	0	0	0	0	0	0	0	0	100	173
£100,000 and under £250,000	1973	0	0	0	0	0	0	0	0	0	0	13	19	100	16
	1965	0	0	0	0	0	5	5	5	5	16	16	37	100	19
	1956–7	0	0	0	0	0	0	0	0	1	4	7	25	100	96
£50,000 and under £100,000	1973	0	0	0	8	8	8	8	17	25	33	58	92	100	12
	1965	0	0	0	0	0	0	0	50	50	60	70	90	100	10
	1956–7	2	3	6	6	8	10	13	16	19	27	42	80	100	64
£25,000 and under £50,000	1973	0	9	9	9	18	18	27	27	27	55	100	100	100	11
	1965	0	0	0	0	8	8	8	17	17	42	83	92	100	12
	1956–7	0	4	14	14	14	18	25	29	54	68	89	100	100	28
£10,000 and under £25,000	1973	0	0	20	33	40	47	60	80	87	100	100			14
	1965	13	13	13	38	50	50	50	63	75	88	100			8
	1956–7	3	3	8	8	16	24	34	50	79	92	100			38
£5,000 and under £10,000	1973	0	67	67	67	67	100	100	100	100	100	100			3
	1965	0	0	0	33	33	67	100	100	100	100	100			3
	1956–7	0	11	17	28	39	56	72	89	95	100	100			18
£1,000 and under £5,000	1973	0	0	17	17	33	50	50	83	100	100	100			6
	1965	33	33	67	67	67	67	100	100	100	100	100			3
	1956–7	21	26	41	56	73	82	85	94	100	100	100			34
Less than £1,000	1973	83	91	100	100	100	100	100	100	100	100	100			23
	1965	38	44	88	88	100	100	100	100	100	100	100			16
	1956–7	53	80	96	96	97	99	100	100	100	100	100			81

conclusions may be drawn for fathers' estate sizes greater than this sum. On the other hand a number of sons previously classified as self-made on the basis of a £25,000 watershed now become inheritors on this new criterion.

The most general conclusion that can perhaps be derived from the table is that of those who were previously described as self-made on the basis of a £25,000 watershed, very roughly one in seven would be described as inheritors (and of those previously described as inheritors very roughly one in twenty would now be described as self-made).

Rates of Accumulation of Sons of Top Male Wealth Leavers of 1902 and 1924–6
Table 3.7 drew attention to the proportions of sons in the samples of 1902 and 1924–6 who might be described as either accumulators or dissipators. Compound interest growth rates have been used in the same way as in the previous section to identify the *rates* of accumulation achieved by sons in the forward tracing samples. The results are shown in Table 3.12.

Growth rates in the forward tracing samples appear at first glance to be substantially below those of the backward tracing samples. The contrast is illusory. All sons in the 1902 and 1924–6 samples had been preceded by fathers who were themselves top wealth leavers. A more realistic comparison of the two types of sample may be obtained by concentrating in Table 3.11 on fathers who left £50,000 and more. Then the proportion of sons in the backward tracing samples having fathers who left more than £50,000 and who achieved at least a 6 per cent rate of growth is 2 per cent (derived from Table 3.11), a result not very different from that obtained for sons of the forward tracing sample.

CHANGES IN THE PRICE LEVEL

The problem of changes in the price level over the period of the entire study has been dealt with so far by means of an index of retail prices which was used to render all estate sizes at constant prices. This is not the only nor necessarily the best method of deflation, and two alternative indices are now considered. These were described in Chapter 2 and are based on asset prices and asset yields. The rationale underlying alternative indices is that each assumes a particular behavioural motivation, and the different effects each has on the data here follow from the fact that not all prices necessarily move together.

Retail Price Index. Use of this index assumes that wealth is held, at least ultimately, for expenditure on goods and services and that the price movements by which fathers' and sons' estates should therefore be adjusted are those of consumer goods and services. The index then renders each individual's wealth to levels corresponding to its sterling purchasing power in 1956–7 regardless of his date of death.

Asset Price Index. The asset price index endows a different motive to

Table 3.12 *Compound Interest Rates Growth Between Sons' Inheritance and Sons' Estates, Fathers Dying in 1902 and 1924–6* (constant prices)

Sample	Cumulative Percentages Growth rate equal to or greater than %												Less than 1	Sample Size
	20	15	10	9	8	7	6	5	4	3	2	1		
Combined 1902 and 1924-6 Samples	1	1	2	2	2	2	4	5	6	7	10	14	100	246

inheritors. Rather than that they wish to spend their wealth on consumption the use of this index implies retention of the inherited assets. It is therefore necessary to compile indices of asset price movements for the adjustment of estate values. Estates are rendered comparable by a weighted index, where the weights are related to the asset composition of the estate. Four groups of assets were considered – cash, land and other realty, ordinary shares and property.[18]

Yield Price Index. The index of asset yields is based on the assumption that inheritors hold wealth in order to derive an income from it. It is the yield of their assets, therefore, by which estates should be adjusted for comparative purposes. Following this behavioural assumption the yield is adjusted to 1956–7 purchasing power by the retail price index. The index is constructed in answer to the question, 'What size of estate in 1956–7 would be required to give an equivalent yield in real terms to that achieved by a father in his year of death?'

The Effects of Using Alternative Indices[19]
The three indices have been applied to the father–son wealth data in the three backward tracing samples of top male wealth leavers for estates since 1900. The effect of the use of the different indices is shown in Table 3.13. The data in the table refer to sons leaving £100,000 or more at prices ruling in the base year 1956–7. Sample size is therefore the same by each index for the 1956–7 sample, but not for the two other sample years because sons' estates in the years 1965 and 1973 are adjusted as well as fathers', and the number of sons whose estates are in excess of £100,000 in 1956–7 values differs according to differences in the indices themselves.

The table is constructed in the same way as Table 3.3,[20] to show the proportions of sons preceded by fathers leaving estates greater than a particular size. Each section of the table refers to one of the three different samples. Within sections are three sets of percentages of sons whose fathers left estates of varying size, each obtained by the application of one of the three indices.[21]

The result of applying the different indices within each sampling year shows that in almost all cases the retail price index values estates the highest, followed by the asset price index and the yield index.

In the earlier analyses, the suggested watersheds for dividing inheritors from the self-made were that their fathers should leave estates of over £10,000, £25,000 or £50,000. Examining the proportions of fathers leaving estates greater than these sums shows a reasonable consistency in proportions, regardless of which index is used. The lesser consistency in the 1965 data reflects the rather smaller (and fluctuating) numbers of individuals included on deflation.

SUMMARY AND CONCLUSIONS

This chapter has examined the father–son wealth relationship for two kinds of samples. That of the 'backward tracing' type showed the

Table 3.13 Estates of Fathers of Top Male Wealth Leavers of 1956–7, 1965 and 1973, Adjusted by Three Price Indices (Base Year 1956–7)

Index	Sample	Size of Father's Estates: Cumulative percentages										Sample Size
		Over £1,000,000	Over £500,000	Over £250,000	Over £100,000	Over £50,000	Over £25,000	Over £10,000	Over £5,000	Over £1,000	All	
RPI	1956–7	9	20	35	55	67	72	79	82	88	100	430
API	1956–7	7	17	32	51	64	70	78	81	88	100	430
YPI	1956–7	5	15	28	50	62	70	77	80	88	100	430
RPI	1965	5	13	24	47	60	74	83	88	91	100	77
API	1965	4	11	29	45	64	76	85	91	96	100	55
YPI	1965	1	7	17	33	46	59	71	81	86	100	118
RPI	1973	6	14	22	40	51	62	76	79	84	100	101
API	1973	3	9	19	37	47	60	72	78	84	100	101
YPI	1973	6	9	20	38	49	59	70	78	84	100	101

Note: RPI is the Retail Price Index, API the Asset Price Index and YPI the Yield Price Index.

importance of fathers' wealth for three samples of sons dying since 1956. At all levels of sons' wealth (between £7,500 and over £500,000 (in 1956–7 prices)) a clear association could be observed between the wealth of the two generations – fathers' wealth increased as sons' estate size class rose – for example, 17 per cent of sons who left estates between £7,500 and £10,000 (in the 1973 sample) were preceded by fathers leaving over £5,000, whereas over 80 per cent of sons leaving in excess of £500,000 were preceded by fathers leaving more than £5,000.

Three issues were considered. First, the proportion of top wealth leavers who might be described as self-made; second, trends in the importance of the father–son wealth relationship this century; and third, the extent to which sons of rich fathers tend to accumulate or to dissipate wealth.

Proportions of Self-made Among the Rich
The first major consideration of this chapter was to determine the relative importance of inheritors to those with self-made wealth. For this it was necessary to adopt criteria for deciding a level of fathers' wealth below which a son could be regarded as self-made. The results based on differing arbitrary criteria are set out in summary form in Table 3.14. The table examines the proportions of persons who may be described as substantial inheritors according to different measures and different arbitrary criteria explained above. Table 3.14(a) shows results based on applying the index of retail prices to the whole data. 3.14(b) deals with the proportions of inheritors according to different price indices. The third and fourth parts of the table examine the same issue on the basis of the growth rate criterion and the relative wealth criterion respectively.

The detailed implications of the different measures for the proportions of individuals in the three samples who may be described as substantial inheritors or self-made are deferred to the concluding chapter. Suffice it to say at this point that although different criteria were tried the most common single arbitrary criterion used is that a son was preceded by a father who had substantial wealth if he left over £25,000. This implies that 58 per cent of the 1973 sample and 68 per cent of the 1965 and 1956–7 samples were substantial inheritors. Such proportions, it can be seen by inspection of Table 3.14, imply a maximum real rate of return of 5 to 6 per cent and that a father's estate would be a multiple of at least 15 times that of the minimum level of wealth of the top 10 per cent in his year of death.

Trends Over Time
The importance of fathers' wealth for substantial wealth leavers (those leaving over £50,000 in 1956–7 prices) did not appear to change greatly between the mid-1920s and the mid-1950s. Thereafter a decline was observable in 1965, which appeared to continue in 1973.

A number of adjustments were made to the data relating to top wealth leavers including the use of three different price index numbers. These did not alter the main conclusions. Likewise a comparison based on the

Table 3.14 *Proportions of Inheritors Among Three Samples of Top Wealth Leavers, 1956–7, 1965 and 1973, According to Different Measures and Different Criteria*

Measure	Criterion		Sample Year								
			1973 %			1965 %			1956–7 %		
			RPI	API	YPI	RPI	API	YPI	RPI	API	YPI
3.14(a) Retail Price Index	Father's Estate										
	greater than £10,000			71			77			75	
	greater than £25,000			58			68			68	
	greater than £50,000			47			55			63	
3.14(b) Different Price Indices	Father's Estate										
	greater than £10,000		76	72	70	83	85	71	79	78	77
	greater than £25,000		62	60	59	74	76	59	72	70	70
	greater than £50,000		51	47	49	60	64	46	67	64	62
3.14(c) Compound Interest Growth Rates	Rate of Growth										
	less than 6%			71			71			71	
	less than 5%			55			63			69	
	less than 4%			53			62			64	
3.14(d) Relative Wealth Index	Father's Wealth as multiple of minimum wealth of Top 10%.	(multiple)									
	more than that of Top 10%*	1		82			91			87	
	5%	3		79			84			81	
	1%	15		60			74			71	

Note: Estates deflated by RPI in 3.14(a) apply to the whole of the data in the three samples. Those estates deflated by RPI in 3.14(b) only apply to fathers dying since 1900 and are therefore not strictly comparable.

* For an explanation of the approximate percentile equivalence see note 15.

position of a father's estate in the distribution of wealth current in his year of death also showed similar general trends of a decline between 1956–7 and 1973 in the proportion of rich sons whose fathers' wealth placed them within the top 10 per cent of wealth leavers.

Finally, similar trends were again observed when compound interest growth rates (measured in real terms) between the size of a father's estate and that of his son over the period of the intergeneration span, were used to quantify the importance of inheritance.

Accumulation and Dissipation

The analysis of the forward tracing samples permitted conclusions to be drawn on the accumulation and dissipation of fortunes. On the assumption of equal division of fathers' estates, approximately two-thirds turned out to be dissipators, leaving less than their share, and one-third accumulators.

NOTES

1 Explanations of the nature of the data and analytical processes are described only briefly here; for full details refer to Chapter 2 above, and in particular Table 2.2, p.12, where the different samples are described. It should be noted that although the wealth of the successors of the 1924–6 sample is considered in this chapter, a number of the predecessors of those dying rich in 1924–6 were also traced, and their wealth is analysed in Chapter 4.

2 These issues have been dealt with in Chapter 2.

3 Duty was not payable on estates of less than £15,000 in 1973, and therefore data at Somerset House are only complete above this level of wealth (and therefore representative of the living population) except where there is a surviving spouse and the limit is raised to £30,000.

4 See Chapter 2, p.28.

5 The statistical test undertaken was the t-test on proportions.

6 See Chapter 2 for a fuller explanation of the categories.

7 See Chapter 2, pp.32–4 for an explanation of how Table 3.6 was constructed.

8 Those proportions which are statistically significantly different are marked with asterisks.

9 Table 3.6 is in current prices. Comparisons of 1973 with 1956–7 involves deflation. Roughly the estate size of £50,000 in 1973 is equivalent to £25,000 in constant prices and the probability is therefore 0·348 per cent.

10 The effect of missing sons' wealth on the findings and comparability with those of the 1902 sample is available as a separate paper from the authors.

11 There is clearly a question of what weights should be given for differing family size and whether to count daughters as well as sons in the calculations. A decision was necessary to keep the amount of work in tabulations minimal unless there were clear and substantial reasons for doing otherwise. The decision taken did not appear to be any less sensible than alternatives. Moreover, in some cases where fathers had no sons nephews have been substituted.

12 The choice of this percentile is arbitrary and makes little difference to the following analysis.

13 Methods of estimating the minima for the years 1900–73 are given in Appendix C.

14 It was not possible to estimate minima for the years before 1900.

15 The proportions of fathers in the top 1 per cent and 5 per cent of the wealth distribution cannot be precisely estimated from Table 3.8, but in view of the nature of the data it is unnecessary to attach any precise significance to the multiples given. The

reason why the minimum wealth of the top 1 per cent and of the top 5 per cent of wealth holders is not a direct multiple of that of the minimum wealth of the top 10 per cent is that the degree of inequality in wealth has changed over time. When inequality is great, for example, the point of entry to the wealth of the top 1 per cent of wealth holders is high, whereas when inequality is less the point of entry will be accordingly lower and proportionally different from that of the top 10 per cent. The distribution of wealth has become more equal this century and hence no single multiple can be applied to the table but the following broad guidance may be given. A multiple of 3 and above will include all fathers within the top 5 per cent of the wealth distribution at their date of death. A multiple of 15 and above will include those in the top 1 per cent.

16 Negative intergeneration spans were precluded by the exclusion of all cases where fathers outlived their sons.

17 The effect of differing intergeneration spans on growth rates is the subject of a separate paper available from the authors.

18 A more detailed account of the method of construction of the indices is given in Appendix C.

19 The three indices themselves are compared in Figure 2.1 (p.31 above).

20 Numbers using RPI differ from Table 3.3 because of truncation by excluding pre-1900 estates.

21 Comparisons between the different sections of Table 3.13 are not justified for two reasons. First, the numbers of fathers included in the analysis differ between the periods – more are left out of the 1956–7 sample than the 1973 sample – and hence affect the randomness of the sub-sample. Second, the sample drawn for 1973 in this analysis is restricted in current prices to sons leaving over £200,000 which is approximately equivalent to £100,000 in 1956–7 by the retail price index. Hence the other indices applied to the 1973 data are already affected by the choice of estate size defining top wealth leavers in 1973.

4

Non-Paternal Sources
of Inheritance

> There is a strange charm in the thoughts of a good legacy,
> or the hopes of an estate, which wondrously alleviates the
> sorrow that men would otherwise feel for the death of
> friends.
>
> Cervantes, *Don Quixote*

The results presented in Chapter 3 were based on the wealth of fathers
and sons. Sources of inheritance are, of course, potentially far wider
than this and it was therefore decided to try to quantify non-paternal
inheritances in this study.

Two approaches may be distinguished. The first is to extend the
matching process in a consistent manner – for example, by tracing the
estates of mothers and fathers-in-law as well as those of the fathers of
top wealth leavers. The advantage of this approach is that it can lead to
the same kind of systematic analysis as that applied to fathers. Its main
disadvantage is that it is inevitably incomplete – since some wealth
passes not only through fathers and fathers-in-law, but also via
nephews, cousins, great-aunts and other more distant relatives. It is
clearly an impossible task to try to trace the wealth of all the relatives of
individuals even in a very small sample of wealth leavers.

The second approach is to take one or two known wealthy families as
case studies and to examine how widely spread their wealth appears to
be. The method has precisely complementary advantages and disadvantages to the first approach. It is not restricted to any particular
relatives, but the search spreads as widely as one chooses to define the
family. However, at the same time there appears to be no way in which
any systematic tools of analysis can be applied to the data.

Analyses using both approaches have been employed here. Systematic
tracing for other relatives was attempted – confined, in the first place, to
the top male wealth leavers of the backward tracing samples – and to
fathers-in-law and mothers. Data are also presented on the wealth of
relatives such as grandfathers, brothers and sisters, aunts and uncles,
from whom individuals in the samples were known to have inherited,
but in these cases the information was either obtained from correspondence or was an incidental outcome of the searching process. Systematic

backward tracing for grandfathers was employed for the 1924–6 sample of top wealth leavers and allows a comparison of the wealth of grandfather, father and son indicating wealth transmission over three generations.

The second approach outlined above provides for a bird's-eye view of the extent to which wealth can extend within a single generation as well as between generations of one family, and highlights the shortcomings of the main method adopted in the bulk of this book of restricting wealth relationships to particular relatives.

THE WEALTH OF FATHERS-IN-LAW

The first exercise was designed with the specific purpose of attempting to quantify non-paternal sources of inheritance of those top wealth leavers who were preceded by relatively poor fathers and who, on that evidence alone, appeared self-made. Searches were carried out for the wealth of the fathers-in-law of the rich sons whose fathers left little wealth to discover whether they had inherited by marrying into a rich family.

The success with which the wealth of fathers-in-law was traced among those identified as self-made (by the earlier analysis) was less than that in the case of fathers because of the great difficulty in establishing a correct marriage certificate and complications of multiple marriages. None the less, for the three samples of 1956–7, 1965 and 1973 the success rates were 72, minimally 83 and 93 per cent, respectively.

THE WEALTH OF FATHERS-IN-LAW AMONG THE SELF-MADE

Table 4.1 compares the wealth of fathers and fathers-in-law for those 'self-made' persons in the three samples of top male wealth leavers. The bench-mark for deciding upon self-made wealth in this analysis is that fathers left less than £25,000 (in 1956–7 prices). The data presented in Table 4.1 compares proportions of fathers leaving estates of varying size below £25,000 with proportions obtained by substituting the higher of fathers' or fathers'-in-law's wealth. For example, the first row in the table shows that 77 per cent of sons were preceded by a father or father-in-law (whichever estate was larger) who left over £1,000, while the second row shows on the basis of the son–father (only) relationship that 52 per cent of 'self-made' sons had fathers leaving more than this amount.

The results show that the importance of inheritance becomes greater if the wealth of fathers-in-law is brought into the picture as well as that of fathers. Moreover, whereas all sons in Table 4.1 would be regarded as self-made on the basis of having been preceded by fathers leaving less than £25,000, it can be seen that some fathers-in-law left more than this level of wealth – 16, 11 and 14 per cent of the 1956–7, 1965 and 1973 samples respectively. However, the total numbers of self-made sons whose fathers-in-law were traced are relatively small, so that the impact of including father-in-laws' wealth is only slight – raising the proportion

Table 4.1   Estates of Fathers and Father's-in-Law of Self-Made* Top Wealth Leavers of 1956–7, 1965 and 1973 (constant prices)

Cumulative Percentages

Father's estate and the higher of father's or father-in-law's estate	Predecessor's Estate Size										Sample Size
	Over £1,000,000	Over £500,000	Over £250,000	Over £100,000	Over £50,000	Over £25,000	Over £10,000	Over £5,000	Over £1,000	All	
Sample 1956–7											
Father/Father-in-law	0	0	0	6	13	16	42	61	77	100	31
Father only	0	0	0	0	0	0	16	26	52	100	31
1965											
Father/Father-in-law	0	6	6	11	11	11	33	39	78	100	18
Father only	0	0	0	0	0	0	28	28	39	100	18
1973											
Father/Father-in-law	0	0	0	3	7	14	38	52	79	100	29
Father only	0	0	0	0	0	0	48	66	69	100	29
Pooled Samples											
Father/Father-in-law	0	1	1	6	10	14	38	53	78	100	78
Father only	0	0	0	0	0	0	24	29	49	100	78

* Self-made sons are defined as those preceded by fathers leaving less than £25,000.

of self-made sons from 34 to 35 per cent when the three samples are combined. In our view marriage was not a very common source of the wealth of those classified here as self-made Top Wealth Leavers. Moreover, some of the few reclassified from self-made to inheritors in in the table on the basis of father-in-law's *wealth*, might have none the less been described as being the sons of upper or upper-middle class fathers. For example, the wealthy (diplomat) son of an Oxford professor who had left some £2,000, married the daughter of a wine-shipper who had left nearly £200,000. Another son, a distiller, whose stock-broker father had left a mere £3,500, took as his (first) wife the daughter of a distiller who had left over a quarter of a million pounds. Two other sons with respectable but relatively poor fathers married Peers of the Realm.

THE IMPORTANCE OF OTHER RELATIVES' WEALTH

It was noted above that in a number of cases the wealth of certain relatives other than fathers and fathers-in-law were traced largely by chance during the process of data collection. They included maternal and paternal grandfathers, uncles, aunts, cousins, brothers and sisters. Table 4.2(a) compares the highest wealth of a predecessor traced, whether it be a father, father-in-law or a grandfather or an aunt etc., with the father–son (only) wealth relationship, and restricts the comparison to just those cases where other predecessors' estates were traced. Hence, 148 predecessors other than fathers were traced in the three samples. Of these the proportion leaving over £250,000 was 24 per cent and this may be compared with the 11 per cent of fathers of the same sub-sample of sons leaving more than this sum.

It can be seen from inspection of the table that substituting the largest estate where a number of predecessors have been traced not unexpectedly raises the importance of inheritance and sets some kind of lower limit to the extent to which the father–son wealth tabulations understate inheritance for top wealth leavers. However, the data contained in Table 4.2 are more illustrative than definitive and cannot because of the way in which they were collected quantify at all precisely the extent to which inheritance rises, even on average, when predecessors other than fathers are included in the analysis. Table 4.2(b) shows the effect on the whole sample when these values are substituted and raises the proportion of sons who had wealthy predecessors in each father's estate size class. This effect is shown graphically in Figure 4.1.

THE RELATIONSHIP BETWEEN FATHERS' WEALTH AND WEALTH OF FATHERS-IN-LAW

A major aspect of the distribution of personal wealth not yet considered is the concentration of wealth within families. A start may be made in assembling data on this matter by examining the relationship between the wealth of husbands and wives. The issue is continued in the next chapter, but this section begins by comparing the wealth of fathers and

Table 4.2 Estates of Fathers and Predecessors of Top Male Leavers of 1956–7, 1965 and 1973 (Pooled) (constant prices). A Comparison of the Wealth of Fathers and that of the Highest Wealth of Predecessors traced among Top Wealth Leavers.

4.2(a)

| | Father's/Highest Predecessor's Wealth: Cumulative Percentages | | | | | | | | | | |
	Over £1,000,000	Over £500,000	Over £250,000	Over £100,000	Over £50,000	Over £25,000	Over £10,000	Over £5,000	Over £1,000	All	Sample Size
Highest Predecessor	8	15	24	38	49	59	70	78	89	100	148
Father only	3	7	11	22	27	36	51	55	66	100	148

4.2(b)

Highest Predecessor	9	19	33	51	64	71	78	83	89	100	734
Father only	8	17	30	48	59	66	75	78	84	100	734

Figure 4.1   *Estates of the fathers and the highest estate of predecessor's wealth traced, 1956–7, 1965 and 1973 (pooled)*
(Percentage of fathers and other predecessors leaving estates in excess of different values)

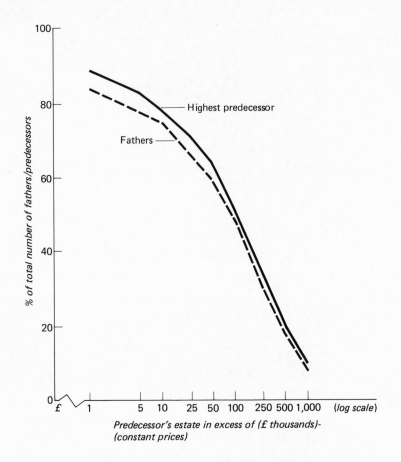

fathers-in-law as indirect evidence of possible concentration.

An exhaustive search was made for fathers-in-law of top wealth leavers dying in 1973. Table 4.3 has been prepared to show the father–father-in-law wealth relationship for those fathers in the sample leaving over £25,000 in constant prices. (Data on the relationship below this level of wealth were given in Table 4.1.) Hence, for example, the first column of the table shows that 21 per cent of sons whose fathers left over £250,000 were associated with fathers-in-law leaving over the same sum. And from the last column it can be seen that 63 per cent of fathers in this sample leaving in excess of £25,000 were associated with fathers-in-law leaving more than this amount. The pattern in the table shows first a relatively strong inverse correlation between fathers' wealth and that of fathers-in-law but a strong probability of fathers-in-law at least being moderately rich.

Table 4.3   *Estates of Fathers and Fathers-in-Law of Top Male Wealth Leavers of 1973 (constant prices)*

Size of Father-in-Law's Estate	Cumulative Percentages Size of Father's Estate			
	Over £250,000	*Over £100,000*	*Over £50,000*	*Over £25,000*
Over £250,000	21	24	19	17
Over £100,000	29	28	22	24
Over £50,000	36	40	38	39
Over £25,000	64	60	63	63
Over £0	100	100	100	100
Sample Size	14	25	32	41

The importance of the wealth of fathers and fathers-in-law among top wealth leavers of 1973 is depicted in Figure 4.2. It can be seen that the wealth of fathers-in-law closely parallels that of fathers but in all cases (because the lines do not cross) fathers' wealth is more important.

MOTHERS' WEALTH

The sources of women's wealth will be considered in detail in Chapter 5. In this section attention is drawn to the wealth of mothers of those rich sons dying in 1973.

The chief importance of mothers in the transmission of wealth is probably that they tend to outlive their husbands and to that extent perhaps delay the time at which a son inherits the capital value of his father's estate. However, two complications have to be considered when comparing the size of the estates of sons, mothers and fathers. First, data on intermarriage among the rich suggest women are likely to inherit and hold wealth also from their fathers, and second, mothers' rights of inheritance from their husbands are frequently limited to life interests in a husband's estate at death [1] and gross probate valuations on a widow's death would not include the full capital from which she may have received an income. For such reasons one would not expect a very clear relationship between the wealth of fathers and that of mothers.

A systematic search for the mothers of the 1973 sample of top male wealth leavers was made, and the importance of mothers' wealth broken down by sons' estate size is shown in Table 4.4. The top four rows of the table show the relationship between sons' estate size and mothers' wealth. The fifth row amalgamates the data and shows the importance of mothers' wealth for all sons leaving over £100,000. Below this is shown, for comparative purposes, the relationship between fathers' and sons' wealth for all cases where mothers' wealth was also traced.

Figure 4.2 *The estates of the fathers and fathers-in-law of top male wealth leavers, 1973*
(Percentages of fathers and fathers-in-law leaving estates in excess of different values)

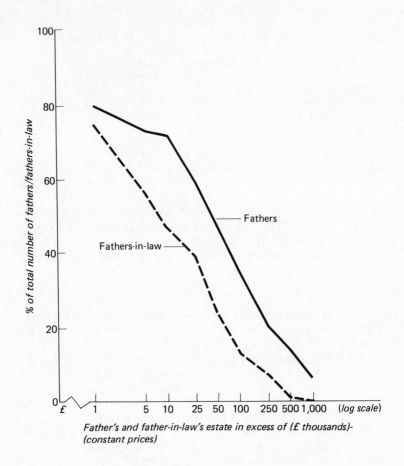

Father's and father-in-law's estate in excess of (£ thousands)-
(constant prices)

The table shows a fairly general tendency for mothers' wealth to be positively associated with sons' estate size class, but the numbers of observations in the cells at the top of the distribution are small. The fifth row of the table shows that some 14 per cent of all mothers traced left estates in excess of £50,000 and 29 per cent in excess of £25,000. These figures may be compared (in Table 4.4(b)) with the 48 and 57 per cent of fathers who left wealth in excess of the same amounts. The father–mother wealth relationship is shown graphically in Figure 4.3. It shows that mothers' wealth is less significant than that of fathers but there is a similar trend in the importance of mothers' wealth.

Table 4.5 extends the analysis of the mother–father wealth relation-

Table 4.4   Estates of Fathers and Mothers of Top Wealth Leavers of 1973 (constant prices)

4.4(a)

Son's Estate Size	Mother's Estate Size: cumulative percentages										Sample Size
	Over £1,000,000	Over £500,000	Over £250,000	Over £100,000	Over £50,000	Over £25,000	Over £10,000	Over £5,000	Over £1,000	All	
Over £500,000	20	20	20	20	20	60	60	100	100	100	5
£300,000 and under £500,000	0	0	0	0	17	50	83	100	100	100	6
£200,000 and under £300,000	0	0	6	6	18	24	59	65	88	100	17
£100,000 and under £200,000	0	0	0	2	12	27	35	50	71	100	68
All over £100,000	1	1*	2*	3*	14*	29*	44*	55*	77	100	96

4.4(b)

	Father's Estate Size: cumulative percentages										
All over £100,000	4	10	19	34	48	57	71	74	80	100	96

* Differences in proportions of sons preceded by rich mothers compared with rich fathers are statistically significantly different at the 5 per cent level.

Figure 4.3 *The estates of the fathers and mothers of top male wealth leavers, 1973*
(Percentages of fathers and mothers leaving estates in excess of different values)

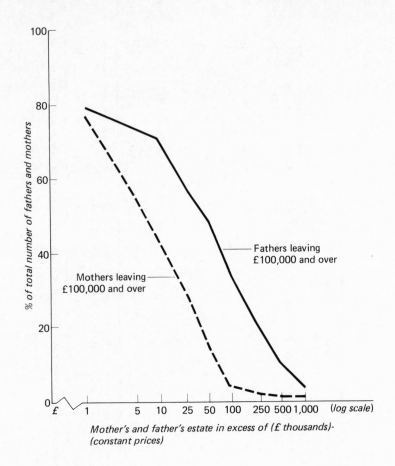

Mother's and father's estate in excess of (£ thousands)-
(constant prices)

ship and compares the size of the estates of fathers with that of mothers. On the vertical column mothers' wealth is subdivided into three wealth size classes and these are compared with the same classes of fathers' wealth. It can be seen, for instance, in the top left hand cell that of those men leaving more than £100,000, 6 per cent of their wives also left estates in the same wealth size class. The table confirms the tendency for mothers' estates at death to be smaller than that of their husbands.

THE INDEPENDENT WEALTH OF MOTHERS

It was argued earlier in this chapter that the relationship between the wealth of fathers and fathers-in-law is likely to be closely bound up with (and indicative of) the joint wealth held by husbands and their wives. The analysis of mothers' wealth has largely been concerned with the question of the transmission of wealth from fathers to their sons, with mothers likely at least to hold a life interest in their husbands' estates before passing wealth on to the next generation.

Table 4.5   *Estates of Fathers and Mothers of Top Male Wealth Leavers of 1973 (constant prices)*

| | Father's Wealth | | |
| | £25,000 | |
Mother's Wealth	*£100,000 and over*	*£25,000 and under £100,000*	*Less than £25,000*
£100,000 and over	6	4	0
£25,000 and under £100,000	61	14	5
Less than £25,000	33	82	95
All	100	100	100
Sample Size	33	22	41

Some mothers of wealthy sons are likely to hold wealth in their own right and it is possible to throw light on the independent wealth of married women by examining the size of estates left by women who predeceased their husbands. Table 4.6 has been prepared for this purpose. The table divides mothers into those who predeceased their husbands shown in the first row and those who outlived their husbands shown in the second row. The third row of the table shows the estates of all mothers in the sample. The nineteen cases missing from the top rows but shown in the bottom row are of those fathers and mothers in the sample whose estates at death were not traced but whose estates are included in the analysis at a notional value. Accordingly it is not possible to distinguish between those who predeceased or outlived their husbands.

It can be seen from the table that the wealth of mothers who predeceased their husbands is less than that of those who outlived their husbands. For example, 13 per cent of mothers in the former category left over £25,000 whereas 44 per cent who survived their husbands left more than this sum.

WEALTH TRANSMISSION OVER THREE GENERATIONS

Analyses so far have been confined to two generations of the same family; however, because of the existence of the practice of 'generation skipping' it was thought important to try to extend the data collection to include a sample of grandfathers, fathers and sons.

The sample of fathers selected for this purpose was that of 1924–6 and grandfathers were traced in 42 of the 55 cases. Choice of this particular sample was influenced by the further possibility of comparing directly

Table 4.6 *Estates of Mothers of Top Male Wealth Leavers of 1973 (constant prices)*

| | Cumulative percentages Size of Mother's Estate | | | | | | | | | | |
	Over £1,000,000	Over £500,000	Over £250,000	Over £100,000	Over £50,000	Over £25,000	Over £10,000	Over £5,000	Over £1,000	All	Sample Size
Predeceased Husband	4	4	4	4	13	13*	30*	44*	99	100	23
Outlived Husband	0	0	2	4	19	44	61	74	93	100	54
All	1	1	2	3	14	29	44	55	77	100	96

* Statistically significant differences from the proportions of those who outlived husband at the 5 per cent level.

Table 4.7 *Estates of Fathers, Grandfathers and Sons, Fathers Dying in 1924–6 and Sons in 1956–7 (constant prices)*

| Father's/Son's Estate Size in Excess of £500,000 | Cumulative percentages Grandfather's/Father's Estate Size | | | | | | | | | | |
	Over £1,000,000	Over £500,000	Over £250,000	Over £100,000	Over £50,000	Over £25,000	Over £10,000	Over £5,000	Over £1,000	All	Sample Size
1924–6 Fathers	21	36	50	62	69	76	83	83	88	100	42
1956–7 Sons	32	40	40	60	76	76	80	80	84	100	25

Note: Each row compares the wealth of two generations. The figures indicate the cumulative percentages of predecessors leaving estates of varying size of two samples of individuals leaving estates in 1924–6 and 1956–7 in excess of £500,000 (constant prices). None of the differences in proportions is statistically significant at the 5 per cent level.

the father–son wealth relationship of the mid-1950s, described in Chapter 3, with that of the mid-1920s.

Table 4.7, then, shows the substantial wealth of grandfathers in the forward tracing sample – 21 per cent left over £1,000,000 and 50 per cent over £250,000. The second row of the table attempts the direct comparison of the father–son wealth relationship for sons of the 1950s with those of 1924–6. Data in the second row include those sons of the 1956–7 sample leaving estates comparable in size with the 1924–6 sample. The extent of the similarity between the percentages of wealthy fathers of the 1956–7 sample of sons and those of the 1924–6 sample of sons can be seen from the table. None of the differences in proportions between the two samples is statistically significant and confirms the earlier findings.

THREE GENERATIONS OF WEALTH HOLDERS

Table 4.8 compares the size of 23 of the 42 grandfathers' estates with 56 of their grandsons. This was the maximum number for which comparisons could be made because others either had no grandchildren or they were still living. For this latter reason the results shown in the table are incomplete and should be treated with caution.

For what it is worth, however, the table shows the relationship between the wealth of grandfathers and that of their grandchildren. Grandfathers' wealth is divided simply into two categories: those leaving less than or more than £50,000. This arbitrary level of wealth was chosen because of the small numbers of grandfathers in the sample – 10 leaving estates of less than £50,000 and 13 whose estates were of more than this sum. (The middle generation (fathers) is excluded since they are all wealthy.) Across the table is shown the wealth of their grandsons at death.

The table shows that any conclusion about whether rich or poor grandsons are more closely associated with rich grandfathers depends on the level of successors' wealth used as a watershed. For grandsons leaving £50,000 or over the association appears to be strongest with poor grandfathers. For grandsons leaving more than £5,000 it is with rich grandfathers. This could conceivably be evidence of generation skipping but since the middle generation (fathers) are all rich, it would be difficult to know how much, if any, generation skipping took place. Further the differences in proportions are not statistically significant and it would be unwise to draw conclusions that the table provides much evidence of a particular pattern of association.

FAMILY WEALTH TREES

This chapter has been concerned to remedy the deficiency implicit in quantifying inheritance by reference to the wealth of fathers and sons. Some evidence has therefore been presented on a systematic basis on the wealth relationship between sons and their mothers, grandfathers and

Table 4.8 *Estates of Grandfathers and Grandsons, Fathers Dying in 1924–6 (constant prices)*

Grandfather's Estate Size	Cumulative percentages Grandson's Estate Size										
	Over £1,000,000	Over £500,000	Over £250,000	Over £100,000	Over £50,000	Over £25,000	Over £10,000	Over £5,000	Over £1,000	All	Sample Size
£50,000 and Less	0	4	22	56	67	74	74	81	93	100	27
Over £50,000	3	10	17	34	55	76	93	97	100	100	29

Note: None of the differences in proportions are statistically significant at the 5 per cent level.

fathers-in-law. Even this is, however, still far from comprehensive because of the exclusion of other and more remote sources of inheritance originating from, for example, grandmothers, uncles, aunts and cousins. In order to illustrate the ways in which wealth may be spread widely or narrowly within families it was decided to construct a 'wealth tree' for one important family as a case study.[2] Such a wealth tree is no more than an ordinary family tree which includes the size of the estates left by members who are dead.

It can hardly be overemphasised that the picture given by any such wealth tree is to a very considerable extent arbitrary. This is because, as any genealogist points out to his clients, there is no such thing as 'a family'; the limits you want to place on it depend on how much time and money you are prepared to spend in extending horizontally in a generation or chronologically backwards in time.[3] No pretence is made, therefore, that the wealth tree for the Wills family presented here can be more than illustrative of the extent to which wealth can pervade branches of a family. No rigorous statistical analysis is possible because any extension (or contraction) of the family tree could completely alter the results of such an exercise. But the trees are presented here, almost as casual empiricism, because we believe they may well be representative of certain socio-economic relationships.

A word might usefully be said about the reason for choosing the Wills' family tree. It mainly is that a family tree had already been published by Alford (1973) in his industrial history of the tobacco industry. So it was possible to rely on the fact that the basic framework from which the trees were constructed was set by a scholar well informed about the family history.[4] The same is true, of course, of a number of other cases, but the Wills' tree was a relatively large one and it so happened that in the course of searching for the father of one member of the family in an early sample, it was noticed that no fewer than ten Wills who died in the first half of the present century left over £2 million.

NOTES

1 The major exceptions are the matrimonial home and chattels.
2 Two other wealth trees were in fact also constructed, for Courtauld and Pilkington, based on the published family trees by Coleman (1969) and Barker (1977). Copies are available from the authors.
3 It is often said that 'we are all (including US President Carter) descended from Edward III', but even if that is not quite true, we are all related to a surprisingly large number of famous people over the ages if we go back far and wide enough.
4 We are most grateful to Dr Alford of the University of Bristol for allowing us to see a most detailed Wills' family tree.

5

Women's Wealth and Marriage

Money ought never to be the consideration in marriage
but it ought always to be a consideration . . . when a man's
doing sums at home evenings, it comes kind of awkward
for him to try to hold his wife on his lap.

George Horace Lorimer, *Letters from a Self-Made
Merchant to his Son* (1903)

The evidence presented so far has been concerned with the importance
of inheritance for men as distinct from women. In this chapter the
sources of the fortunes of wealthy women are considered with particular
reference to the relative positions of fathers and husbands in the process
of wealth transmission. The extent of intermarriage among the wealthy
is further considered as is also the importance of self-made wealth
among women.

TRENDS IN WOMEN'S WEALTH SHARES

Women's share in total personal wealth has risen since the 1920s both in
the United Kingdom and in the United States (Revell, 1965; Atkinson
and Harrison, 1978; Lampman, 1962). By the mid-1950s women owned
approximately 40 per cent of the total in each country, though there
have since been signs of a reversal of this trend (Diamond, 1975; Smith,
1974). Women's wealth exhibits a number of other characteristics
common to the two countries. Wealth distribution tends to be more
unequal among women than among men and inequality is greatest
among lower age groups for female wealth holders. The asset composition of estates differ between men and women, but both in Britain
and in the United States women hold higher proportions of their assets
in stock-market securities (both equities and bonds), in deposits in
building societies and in cash; and lower proportions in real estate,
shares in unquoted companies and trade and professional assets.

The upward trend in women's share of wealth can be explained by the
increasing tendency for spouses to hold property jointly and by the
division of wealth within families for tax purposes.[1] The trend has also
been attributed to demographic changes, especially women's increasing

longevity. But the importance of this factor is influenced by the rate of increase in life expectancy since the beginning of the century which is remarkably similar for men and women (Benjamin, 1968). Any explanation of changing shares based on official statistics must, however, be viewed with caution. Social trends in the use of gifts and trusts as tax avoidance devices, which are excluded from Inland Revenue valuations, will be reflected in the data. For example, because the majority of gifts are made by men rather than by women[2] and the volume of giving has been increasing, the statistics should therefore show some rise in women's share of personal wealth.

There has been a decline since 1960 in women's share which is perhaps surprising in view of the rapid rise in the divorce rate and the increasingly favourable attitude to women shown by the courts in the division of property. It has been suggested that the major cause of the decline is again a demographic one arising from the imbalance between the sexes after the First World War when a large proportion of women remained single or were widowed early – an imbalance which has gradually been disappearing. Two other possible explanations of this decline are worthy of note although neither can be substantiated or refuted on the basis of information available at the present time. The first is that women may have lagged behind men in the adoption of tax planning and to that extent their changing share would be partly illusory. The second explanation is that women have tended to hold a disproportionate amount of their wealth in the form of assets whose capital value has appreciated relatively little.

The evidence presented here on women's wealth relates to the predecessors of a sample of 140 women leaving estates valued for probate in 1973 at over £200,000 (referred to as TFWH).[3] An attempt was made to trace the estates left by the fathers of all of them as well as of husbands and fathers-in-law of the 101 who had married. In the event, after the elimination of 42 predecessors who were still alive or who had lived or died abroad, fathers and husbands were traced in 91 and 99 per cent of cases.

THE WEALTH OF FATHERS

Table 5.1 shows the importance of fathers' wealth in constant 1956–7 prices for top female wealth leavers. The table shows three categories of women's wealth and the estates left by their fathers.[4] It can be seen, for example, that of those rich females leaving over £300,000, 11 per cent were preceded by fathers leaving more than £500,000, 44 per cent by fathers leaving more than £250,000, and so on. The table shows the general tendency for fathers' wealth to be positively associated with that of their daughters. If the column of fathers' wealth of over £100,000 is examined it can be seen that 89 per cent of fathers left wealth in excess of this in the top women's estate size class, 67 per cent in the middle and 50 per cent in the lowest estate size class of their daughters. The last two rows in Table 5.1 distinguish spinsters and married women. As might be expected fathers' wealth is more important for the former than for the latter for all but the lowest size class of fathers' estates, and a number of the differences in proportions are statistically significantly different. For example, 69 per cent of all spinsters leaving £100,000 or more were themselves preceded by fathers leaving more than the same amount, compared with only 49 per cent of married women. No less than 81 per cent of top unmarried female wealth leavers had fathers leaving over £50,000, as against 59 per cent of married women (and 47 per cent of men). The greater importance of fathers' wealth for spinsters among female top wealth leavers highlights the probable importance of husbands' wealth.

It is of some interest to compare the father–daughter wealth relationship in Table 5.1 with the same relationship between fathers and sons for the same year. This is done in Figure 5.1 which relates to successors classed as top wealth leavers for 1973. It can be seen from the graph that the fathers of rich women tended to be richer than those of rich men over almost the entire distribution. The curve representing the cumulative percentages of the fathers of the female wealth holders leaving estates above various sizes is quite clearly above and to the right of that for rich males dying in 1973. They cross only at the extreme top of the distribution for fathers leaving over £500,000, implying that fewer rich women than men were preceded by millionaire fathers, but the numbers in these cells are too small to be reliable.

THE WEALTH OF HUSBANDS

Table 5.2 shows the estates left by husbands who predeceased their wives. The general tendency for predecessors' wealth to be positively associated with that of successors noted in the case of fathers of both sons and of daughters is again observable for these rich women. Concentrating on the last summary row of the table it can be seen that 33 per cent of all married female top wealth leavers were preceded by husbands leaving over £100,000, 47 per cent by husbands leaving over £50,000 and 63 per cent by husbands leaving more than £25,000.

THE WEALTH OF FATHERS AND HUSBANDS

The number of rich female wealth leavers who can be said to have come from and/or married into wealthy families clearly depends upon how one defines 'wealthy'. If the figure is set at the minimum estate size by which the women are classed as rich (£100,000), then roughly half the women in the sample had rich fathers and a third had rich husbands. However, if the minimum bench-mark of £25,000 used earlier is taken then it can be seen from Tables 5.1 and 5.2 that 72 and 63 per cent of all rich women were preceded by rich fathers and rich husbands respectively. These figures may be compared with those for men – 58 per cent of top male wealth leavers in 1973 had rich fathers. As previously noted, a higher proportion (84 per cent) of rich spinsters, however, had rich fathers.

Table 5.1 *Estates of Fathers and Daughters Dying in 1973 (constant prices)*

Status	Size of Woman's Estate	Size of Father's Estate: cumulative percentages										
		Over £1,000,000	Over £500,000	Over £250,000	Over £100,000	Over £50,000	Over £25,000	Over £10,000	Over £5,000	Over £1,000	All	Sample Size
All Women	£300,000 and over	0	0	44	89	100	100	100	100	100	100	9
	£200,000 and under £300,000	0	11	42	67	67	75	83	83	83	100	12
	£100,000 and under £200,000	5	33	27	50	61	69	78	79	87	100	96
	Over £100,000	4	15	30	55	65	72	80	81	88	100	117
Spinsters	Over £100,000	6	16	34	69	81*	84*	94*	97*	97	100	32
Married Women	Over £100,000	4	16	28	49	59	67	75	75	85	100	85

Note: Data presented in this table first appeared in the *Economic Journal*, March 1977. It should be noted that percentages in this table differ from those published formerly and are in constant 1956–7 prices, not 1973 prices as formerly presented.
* Statistically significantly different at the 5 per cent level from the proportions of married women preceded by fathers leaving estates of varying size.

Table 5.2 *Estates of Husbands and Wives Dying in 1973 (constant prices)*

Size of Woman's Estate	Size of Husband's Estates: cumulative percentages										
	Over £1,000,000	Over £500,000	Over £250,000	Over £100,000	Over £50,000	Over £25,000	Over £10,000	Over £5,000	Over £1,000	All	Sample Size
£300,000 and over	0	20	40	60	60	60	80	100	100	100	5
£200,000 and under £300,000	0	0	14	29	43	86	100	100	100	100	7
£100,000 and under £200,000	0	2	3	31	47	60	81	84	95	100	58
Over £100,000	0	3	7	33	47	63	83	87	96	100	70

Figure 5.1   *The estates of the fathers of top male and female wealth leavers, 1973 (Percentage of fathers leaving estates in excess of different values)*

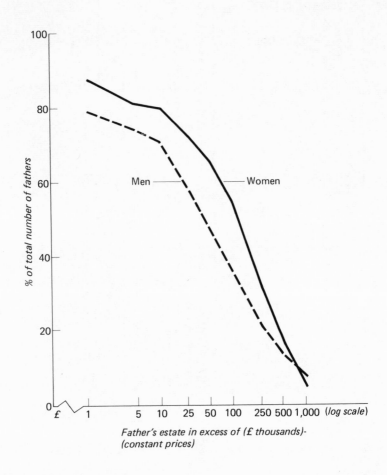

Tables 5.1 and 5.2 do not show the number of women in the sample who were preceded *both* by rich fathers and by rich husbands. This information is presented in Table 5.3 which shows the percentages of all pairs of the two predecessors who left estates of varying size. Thus 8 per cent of husbands who left less than £25,000 were associated with fathers of women who also left less than £25,000. Adding relevant percentages in cells and using the £25,000 watershed, it can be seen that 40 per cent of women had both a rich father and a rich husband, 68 per cent had just a rich father, and 63 per cent just a rich husband.

'SELF-MADE' WOMEN

Table 5.3 shows that 92 per cent, or all but five of the sixty rich women in

Table 5.3   *Estates of Fathers and Husbands of Top Female Wealth Leavers of 1973 (constant prices)**

	Husband's Wealth				
Father's Wealth	£100,000 and over	£50,000 £99,999	£25,000 £49,999	Less than £25,000	Sample Size
£100,000 and over	13	5	8	22	29
£50,000–£99,999	2	2	3	3	6
£25,000–£49,999	5	0	2	3	6
Less than £25,000	13	7	3	8	19
				Total	60

* Figures in each cell are percentages of total observations in the table.

the 1973 sample, had rich fathers or husbands, or both. One is however less justified in assuming, as in the case of men, that the remaining 8 per cent were 'self-made'. Including spinsters, there were ten women in the entire sample of 117 who did not have any predecessor (father or husband) who left more than £25,000. Estates and occupations of these individuals and their predecessors are listed in Table 5.4. The top half of the table shows the wealth of spinsters and that of their fathers and the occupations of both. The bottom half of the table shows the same data for married women.

Several of these women were the children or daughters of men of modest wealth, though leaving less than £25,000. If one takes account of the occupations listed and the importance of inheritances from other relatives, our judgement is that no more than four or five of the women could seriously be considered 'self-made'. We happen to know from correspondence that one woman built her fortune from property development, while another received some shares from a millionaire.[5]

THE WEALTH OF FATHERS-IN-LAW

In addition to the collection of data on the wealth of the fathers and husbands of top female wealth leavers, information was also obtained of the estates left by the fathers-in-law of those who had been married. Table 5.5 shows the cumulative percentages of women who were associated with fathers-in-law leaving estates of varying size. It shows that almost exactly half had fathers-in-law leaving more than £25,000, a proportion that may be compared with the 63 and 67 per cent having husbands and fathers leaving estates above that size respectively.

Figure 5.2 shows the association between the wealth of the women in the sample and that of their fathers, husbands and fathers-in-law. It can be seen from the graph that the wealth of fathers appears the most important, followed by that of husbands and then that of fathers-in-law.

Table 5.4 *Estates of Fathers, Husbands and Fathers-in-Law of Married Women and Spinsters Dying in 1973 (constant prices)*

Spinsters		Fathers	
*Occupation**	*Estate Size*	*Occupation**	*Estate Size*
Doctor	£104,000	Clergyman	£ 8,544

Spinsters		Fathers	
*Occupation**	*Estate Size*	*Occupation**	*Estate Size*
Doctor	£126,000	Clergyman	£ 8,544
Farmer	£127,000	Farmer	£20,271
NS	£112,000	Farmer	£12,171
Private Means	£268,000	Corset manufacturer	£23,698
Private Means	£122,000	Gunmaker	£18,092

Married Women		Father		Husband		Father-in-law	
*Occupation**	*Estate Size*	*Occupation*	*Estate Size*	*Occupation*	*Estate Size*	*Occupation*	*Estate Size*
NS	£104,000	Missionary	£7,299	Ladies' garment manufacturer	£5,963	Coat manufacturer	NV‡
NS	£107,000	Master-grocer	£7,394	Grocer	£11,112	Domestic chef	NV
NS	£111,000	Carpenter	NV	Bootmaker	NV	Clerk	£484
NS	£156,000	Shoemaker	£591	Accountant	£1,539	Pewterer	NV
NS	£116,000	Post Office official	NV	Army captain	£996	Engineer in Royal Navy/ Rear Admiral	£11,889

* *Source:* Death and/or marriage certificates.
NS = Not stated on death or marriage certificate.
NV = Notional value (less than £1,000) (see pp.17–8).
‡ Evidence in this case was based on correspondence with relatives of the deceased.

Table 5.5 *Estates of Fathers-in-Law of Top Female Wealth Leavers of 1973 (constant prices)*

Woman's Estate Size	Size of Father-in-Law's Estate: cumulative percentages										Sample Size
	Over £1,000,000	Over £500,000	Over £250,000	Over £100,000	Over £50,000	Over £25,000	Over £10,000	Over £5,000	Over £1,000	All	
All over £100,000	3	3	13	27	41	49	63	71	84	100	79

Table 5.6 *Estates of Fathers and Husbands of Top Female Wealth Leavers of 1973 (constant prices)*

Husband's Estate Size	Father's Estate Size: cumulative percentages				Sample Size
	Over £100,000	Over £50,000	Over £25,000	All	
£100,000 and over	44	50	67	100	18
£25,000 and under £100,000	35	53	59	100	17
Less than £25,000	4	13	17	100	23

Figure 5.2   *The estates of the fathers, husbands and fathers-in-law of top female wealth leavers, 1973*
(Percentages of fathers, husbands and fathers-in-law leaving estates in excess of different values)

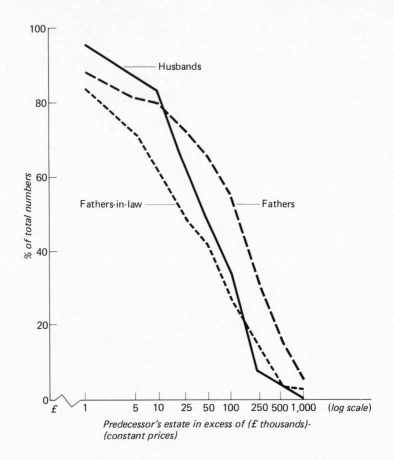

HUSBANDS' AND FATHERS' WEALTH

The relationship between husbands' and fathers' wealth is shown in Table 5.6, which is set out on the usual lines. It shows, for example, that about two-thirds of husbands leaving more than £100,000 were preceded by fathers whose wealth was in excess of £25,000. The pattern in the table is not dissimilar to that of Table 3.2 though the tables are not strictly comparable.[6] In line with earlier tables, fathers' wealth is seen to tend to rise as husbands' wealth size class increases, though the number of husbands coming from relatively modest backgrounds who married into wealth is not inconsiderable.

INTERMARRIAGE AMONG THE RICH

The previous sections provide a basis from which one may begin to answer the question about how far the rich tend to marry among one another. Evidence on the extent of assortative mating is of major importance in the appreciation and quantification of social mobility. Assortative mating for social characteristics such as social class has been reported to be strongest at the top end of the class scale.[7] Particular interest attaches, therefore, to the extent of intermarriage within the highest wealth groups.

A first approach to this subject was made in Chapter 4, where the relationship between the wealth of fathers and of fathers-in-law of the sample of top male wealth leavers for 1973 was presented (see above, Table 4.3) and which throws some light on the extent to which the *sons* of the rich marry *daughters* from different wealth classes. Complementary information consists of evidence on which the *daughters* of the rich marry *sons* from different wealth categories. This information is supplied in Table 5.7 which shows the association between the wealth of the fathers and the fathers-in-law of the sample of rich women dying in 1973. The evidence from the male sample is repeated alongside that of the female sample for purposes of comparison; though not in order to reveal different marriage patterns between the sexes. If the tables were based upon data for the entire population each should tell the same story – one being merely the mirror image of the other. They differ because each is based upon a particular sample of rich men and of rich women with its own distinct distribution of dates of marriage. Nevertheless, the percentages in the corresponding cells in the tables for men and for women are sufficiently close to afford some indication of the likely range within which intermarriage takes place among those in the highest wealth groups.[8]

Measurement of the strength of the forces making for men and women to marry within their own wealth class depends, of course, on the decisions taken about the limits of the wealth size classes. If one takes the lower limit of £25,000 as the bench-mark above which an individual is termed rich, then about three-fifths of both sons and daughters of rich fathers married into rich families (i.e. had rich fathers-in-law). Furthermore, the percentage of the children of either sex with wealthy fathers marrying into equally wealthy families tends to decline as fathers' estate class rises.

MOTHERS' WEALTH

An analysis of the wealth of the mothers of top male wealth leavers was included in Chapter 4. The main conclusion arising therefrom was that the wealth of mothers who were also widows was substantially greater than that of those who predeceased their husbands. No direct comparisons are possible between the wealth of the independent sample of female wealth holders just examined and that of the mothers of the previous chapter. The former sample is a particular one of women

Table 5.7   *Estates of Fathers and Fathers-in-Law of Top Male and Top Female Wealth Leavers of 1973* (constant prices)*

Size of father-in-law's estate	Size of Father's Estate			
	Over £250,000 %	*Over £100,000* %	*Over £50,000* %	*Over £25,000* %
	(a) Women's Sample			
Over £250,000	11	15	17	15
Over £100,000	28	27	27	30
Over £50,000	50	48	49	49
Over £25,000	67	58	56	57
Over £0	100	100	100	100
Sample size	18	33	41	47
	(b) Men's Sample			
Over £250,000	21	24	19	17
Over £100,000	29	28	22	24
Over £50,000	36	40	38	39
Over £25,000	64	60	63	63
Over £0	100	100	100	100
Sample size	14	25	32	41

* In view of the great difficulty in identifying marriage certificates it was not possible to treat separately persons marrying more than once. In those cases where multiple marriages were found their exclusion did not materially affect the results.

leaving £100,000 and over at 1956–7 prices. The latter set of mothers covered the entire wealth scale, the numbers leaving more than the minimum to qualify as top wealth leavers being very small indeed.

CONCLUSIONS

The conclusions which can be drawn from this chapter on women's wealth are, first, that the sources of women's property are their husbands and fathers. Only a very small minority (no more than 5 per cent) accumulated their wealth through what is generally regarded as entrepreneurship. And, second, that approximately 60 per cent of rich sons (daughters) of rich fathers marry daughters (sons) from wealthy families.

NOTES

1   See Diamond (1975), p. 105, for a number of explanations of trends in women's shares. Changing social attitudes to the use of marriage settlements in favour of women is also likely to affect these trends. Further note that the ratio of women to men among top wealth holders in community property states in the USA has been about one-third higher than for the nation as a whole. See Lampman (1962), p. 102.
2   The importance of this factor can only be determined in the light of information on the

sex distribution of gifts; see Horsman (1975).

3   For details of this sample see Chapter 2, pp.12–13. Further, it should be remembered that all tabulations in constant prices are on the basis of those ruling in 1956–7.

4   It should be noted that the limitations of probate valuations as proxies for personal wealth holdings tend to be greater and to understate wealth more for women than for men.

5   Whether the latter case is classified as inheritance or entrepreneurship is left to the reader to decide.

6   This is because husbands who may be compared with sons in Table 3.2 died over an extended period of time and are not to be compared with any particular sample of wealth leavers drawn in those analyses.

7   Correlation coefficients have been reported of a wide range of physical and other characteristics of mating couples (Colman, 1977).

8   A χ test between rows and columns in Table 5.7(a) and (b) revealed no statistically significant differences between them at the 5 per cent probability level. The numbers in several of the cells are, however, small.

6

The Characteristics of
Wealth Leavers

It requires a great deal of boldness and a great deal of
caution to make a great fortune, and when you have got
it, it requires ten times as much wit to keep it.

Emerson, 'Power', *The Conduct of Life*, 1860

The previous three chapters have been largely concerned with the
quantification of inheritance this century. The present chapter, in
contrast, is devoted to an analysis of the characteristics of persons
identified as inheritors as distinct from self-made men.

The background information about the individuals included in the
samples is inevitably limited. A great deal is known about some of the
prominent people whose dates of death brought them into the study
(such as Sir Winston Churchill and Viscountess Leverhulme), but it is
important to avoid the obvious bias resulting from the use of only the
rather small number of persons about whom details of their lives are
known. Hence the analysis that follows is restricted to the four[1]
characteristics for which data are available for the great majority of men
in the samples (sex has been considered in Chapter 5):

(1) Location
(2) Status
(3) Occupation
(4) Age.

The question arises as to whether it is legitimate to amalgamate data
over more than one sample in order to minimise the problem of drawing
conclusions based on relatively few observations.

The data cover an extended period of time and it has been noted that
some of the differences in proportions between the samples of top wealth
leavers in 1956–7 and 1973 were statistically significant. Nevertheless,
the three samples of decedents in 1956–7, 1965 and 1973 cover a period
of fifteen to twenty years in the third quarter of the present century and it
was felt that any trends occurring within this relatively short period
could be ignored, and they are amalgamated. Together they produce a
total of more than 700 observations of father–son relationships and
form the basis of the analysis.

LOCATION

Information is available in the Probate Calendars of the address of the deceased. The original intention of the study was to include residence as a variable according to which father's wealth might be analysed. However, it transpired that a large number of top wealth leavers resided in places other than those where they had worked, for example at seaside resorts and other places of retirement. It was therefore felt that such data could not usefully be used to throw light on the relative importance of inheritance in different parts of the country.

Scottish Wealth

There was one area where information about residence appeared to be reasonably reliable. This was Scotland. Separate Scottish Calendars are available and they provide a workable means of identifying Scottish wealth holders. It should be made clear that this is not the same as Scottish *wealth*. Residents of England and Wales who own immovable property in Scotland need to have their grants 'resealed' in Scotland but the value thereof is included in their English estate. Likewise decedents in the Scottish Calendar are credited with the value of any English realty in the total of their estate.

The Distribution of Wealth in Scotland

The Inland Revenue estimates of the distribution of wealth by region indicate that wealth is more unequally distributed in Scotland than in England and Wales. Estimates of wealth holdings for four quantile groups are given in Table 6.1 for the year 1975. It should be noted that the criterion used by the Inland Revenue to allocate wealth holders by region is close to, but not identical with, that for probate purposes referred to in the previous paragraph.[2]

Table 6.1   *Distribution of Wealth in England/Wales and Scotland, 1975*

| | Percentage share of wealth | |
Quantile group (cumulative)	England and Wales %	Scotland %
Top 1 per cent	22·9	27·3
Top 5	45·8	52·8
Top 10	61·6	68·0
Top 20	81·1	85·6

Source: Inland Revenue Statistics (Series B).

The figures should be regarded with some care in so far as the basis on which they are prepared is not identical in the two countries. The number of estates on which estimates are based is much smaller in Scotland than England and Wales. Further the proportion of missing wealth holders is slightly greater in Scotland though not as great as in previous years when Scottish wealth inequality was estimated to be much greater than in 1975. Nevertheless, the table still shows a tendency for the degree of wealth inequality to be greater in Scotland (the top 5 per cent of wealth holders owned approximately 53 per cent compared with 46 per cent in England and Wales).

Inheritance in Scotland
The question arises as to whether the apparently greater Scottish wealth inequality is matched by a greater importance of inheritance in the distribution of wealth in Scotland.[3] A sample was therefore drawn from the Scottish Calendars of top wealth leavers dying in 1965. This year was chosen as being the closest comparable with any of the recent samples of estates analysed in Chapter 3. (Estates after 1967 are not indexed in the same way as those for England and Wales. In particular the size of the estate is not included so that a comparison with the data drawn for 1973 would have been possible only at an extremely high time cost.)

The two samples for 1965 are compared in Table 6.2 in which various sizes of sons' estates are compared with the cumulative percentages of fathers leaving estates of different sizes. The table compares the father–son wealth relationship for all sons leaving £100,000 or more at current prices of that year. All estates are converted to the basis of the usual 1956–7 prices. They refer then to estates of approximately over £80,000 at constant 1956–7 prices.

Using the arbitrary bench-mark of £25,000 used in earlier chapters to separate inheritors from the self-made, the figures in Table 6.2 show that precisely the same 68 per cent of men leaving £100,000 or more were preceded by 'rich' fathers in both countries. A higher bench-mark – £50,000 – suggests inheritance to be less important in Scotland, but a still higher one – £100,000 – yields exactly the reverse conclusion. Moreover, none of the individual differences in proportions is statistically significant. Hence, on the basis of this sample of Scottish wealth leavers the relationship which exists between wealth and inheritance cannot be said to differ from that existing in England and Wales.

STATUS

Status can be measured by the use of a number of proxies, the most common of which is social class. Attempts were therefore made to allocate individuals in the samples used here to one or other of the main categories on the basis of standard criteria. The exercise was abandoned at an early stage because the data available for the determination of the social class, as distinct from the wealth class, of individuals proved to be quite inadequate in the majority of cases.

However, there was one unambiguous criterion that did enable the dichotomisation of the individuals in the samples that appeared to have some fairly clear connection with status. This was whether or not a person was listed in one of the standard directories employed in the

Table 6.2 Estates of Fathers and Sons, Top Wealth Leavers of 1965 in Scotland and England and Wales (constant prices)

Son's Estate Size	Sample	Father's Estate Size: cumulative percentages										Sample Size
		Over £1,000,000	Over £500,000	Over £250,000	Over £100,000	Over £50,000	Over £25,000	Over £10,000	Over £5,000	Over £1,000	All	
£100,000 and over	Scotland	9	23	31	40	43	68	71	80	83	100	35
	England & Wales	4	12	24	45	55	68	77	80	83	100	94
£80,000 and under £100,000	Scotland	0	0	6	33	44	56	61	61	78	100	18
	England & Wales	0	2	13	27	36	42	58	65	80	100	45
All over £80,000	Scotland	6	15	23	38	43	64	68	74	81	100	53
	England & Wales	3	9	21	39	49	60	71	75	82	100	139

Note: None of the differences in proportions between the two areas is statistically significant at the 5 per cent level.

search for fathers' names: *Who's Who, Burke's Peerage, Burke's Landed Gentry, Debrett's,* and *Kelly's Directory of the Titled, Landed and Official Classes.* Those who appeared are for convenience dubbed 'VIPs'.

VIPs

Persons whose names appeared in one of the five principal directories could be said, in a sense, to have achieved a special status in that they had been recognised by the world of directory editors. Some interest attaches therefore to the question of whether they happen to be associated with higher or lower proportions of predecessors who might be classed as rich.

Table 6.3 compares the father–son wealth relationship for VIPs as defined above with that for all top wealth leavers for the three sample years 1956–7, 1965 and 1973. The following analysis is based on a pooling of the three samples. No attempt is made to draw conclusions on trends between the 1950s and 1970s[4] and the figures throw light on the situation as it existed in the twenty years up to 1973.

The rows in Table 6.3 refer to four distinguishable categories of VIPs: Peers of the Realm, persons cited in *Burke's Landed Gentry*, Knights Bachelor and those mentioned only in *Who's Who* or *Kelly's Handbook of the Titled, Landed and Official Classes.* The bottom row of the table shows the father–son relationship for all top wealth leavers in the samples. It is of course true that comparisons between each sub-group and the remainder of the sample are statistically preferable. However, in view of the large number of observations it was thought justifiable and convenient to have a single universal bench-mark for the purpose of the numerous comparisons in this chapter.[5]

The results show that the cumulative percentages of sons whose fathers left estates of varying size are greater for those appearing in each of the directories than for the population of top wealth leavers as a whole. As might be expected the importance of inheritance for Peers of the Realm and persons cited in *Burke's Landed Gentry* is markedly greater than that for the full sample of top wealth leavers. Indeed, approaching two-thirds of these two groups had fathers who had left more than a quarter of a million pounds, roughly double that for the whole population in the study. A similar result is true for the much larger category of VIPs covered by *Who's Who* and *Kelly's Handbook of the Titled, Landed and Official Classes,* which includes almost all those in the previous two categories. For example, one-half of these VIPs had fathers leaving more than £250,000, compared with less than one-third for all top wealth leavers. Surprisingly, perhaps, the category of Knights Bachelor is unique in that it shows a father–son wealth relationship which is least dissimilar from that of the population of top wealth leavers taken as a whole. One hesitates to offer an explanation of this result without more detailed research. It does suggest, however, that recent generations of sons leaving £100,000 and over were not more likely to be knighted simply because they had wealthy fathers. Perhaps prime

Table 6.3 *Estates of Fathers and Sons, Top Male Wealth Leavers, VIPs (constant prices)*

| | Father's Estate Size: cumulative percentages | | | | | | | | | | |
	Over £1,000,000	Over £500,000	Over £250,000	Over £100,000	Over £50,000	Over £25,000	Over £10,000	Over £5,000	Over £1,000	All	Sample Size
Burke's Peerage	30*	45*	64*	84*	87*	91*	93*	93*	95*	100	56
Burke's Landed Gentry	23*	48*	60*	80*	87*	90*	93*	93*	94*	100	88
Kelly's/Who's Who	18*	35*	50*	68*	81*	87*	90*	91*	94*	100	220
Knights	13	18	37	55	66	74	76	79	87	100	38
All top wealth leavers	8	17	30	48	59	66	75	78	84	100	734

* Statistically significantly different at the 5 per cent level from that of the total sample data.

ministers have not been greatly influenced in creating knighthoods by a person's financial background.

OCCUPATION

The second characteristic of individuals in the sample about whom information was available was that of their occupations. The sources of data were many and various, the principal ones being directories, death and marriage certificates, wills, entries in the *Directory of Directors* and correspondence with relatives. In order to minimise problems of demarcation between concepts of occupational and industrial groupings the basis used for classification was the Standard Industrial Classification (SIC) which treats professions as a separate order. Since the largest sample is that of 1956–7, the 1958 version of the SIC was used for coding purposes. Inevitably some allocatory decisions were more or less arbitrary, but it proved eventually possible to classify some 90 per cent of the sample. An additional class (referred to as XXV) was created for sons with multiple directorships. However, it may be that several allocated to XXV might have been better added to SIC XXI (insurance, banking and finance) but none the less had several other directorships. An example may help to explain the procedure. One lawyer, banker (and politician) who was chairman and particularly associated with one company, in SIC XV, but who was also a director of five other companies including a bank and a colliery, was classed in category XXV, while another person, styled as a financier, who was a director of a dozen companies, was put in SIC XXI. Those about whose occupation the only record was 'of independent means' on their death certificate, were not included in this part of the study. The aim in this section is to identify individual SICs and combinations of these where inheritance appears to have been relatively important.

Inheritance and the Occupations of Wealth Leavers – Method of Analysis
Before turning to examine the results, it is necessary to face the problem of the small number of observations obtained in a number of cells. Given twenty-five SICs and ten wealth size classes for predecessors, it is clear that tabulations are bound to cover several cells with very small and even zero numbers of observations. It has been decided, therefore, to restrict data on each individual class of SIC to cases where a minimum of ten observations were obtained.

The analysis which follows applies only to those *top* male wealth leavers of the three backward tracing samples. Classifications based on SIC only approximate occupations and since it is the purpose of this section to throw light on those industrial groupings most likely to be associated with self-made as compared with inherited wealth, such a broad classification is only applied here to the very rich.

Sons' Occupations

Table 6.4 shows the relationship between sons' occupations and inheritance. The rows refer to different SICs, the final row in the table shows the relationship between wealth and inheritance for the whole sample of wealth leavers. Reading across the table data are given on the cumulative percentages of sons in any particular SIC whose fathers left varying sizes of estates. Hence, for example, row 1 which refers to Agriculture, forestry and fishing, shows that of those 84 sons classified in this occupation 14 per cent were preceded by fathers who were millionaires. This percentage may be compared with that for the population of sons shown in the bottom row of the table, where 8 per cent were preceded by fathers leaving estates of over £1 million. Indeed, the method of analysis may be explained if we proceed by comparing the data on the importance of inheritance for those involved in each SIC group with that of all top male wealth leavers dying over the period.

It can be seen from the comparison that the percentages of sons whose fathers left estates of varying sizes is greater in agriculture than for the population of sons taken as a whole in all fathers' wealth groups. It may be concluded then, perhaps unsurprisingly, that inheritance is relatively more important in agriculture. Similar comparisons are possible for other SICs shown in the table with a view to separating those industries which are more strongly associated with inheritance from those associated with self-made wealth.

Seven industry groups appear to favour inheritors. These are Agriculture, Food, drink and tobacco, Metal manufacture, Textiles, Distribution, Professions, and Public administration. Those, on the other hand, which tend to favour the self-made are Chemicals, Metal goods n.e.s. Clothing, Paper printing, Construction, Transport, Finance, Miscellaneous services, and those with multiple interests. Many, but not all, have the stamp of statistical significance.

An alternative method of making this comparison is shown in Table 6.5 where SICs are classified into the two groups according to tendencies of an association with inherited or self-made wealth. The results show a much stronger dichotomy between the two groups and nearly all proportions are statistically significantly different both between groups and from the total sample data shown in the bottom row.

Caution is necessary for fear of deducing too much from the dichotomy, but it is interesting to note that the split favouring those with inheritances as against the self-made does not appear to coincide with a division between old and new industries (Rubenstein, 1971). The division is, perhaps, to one containing a relatively large or small number of small firms. There are, of course, exceptions to this. The only reasonable conclusion to be drawn is that the creation of sizeable fortunes by individuals mentioned in the self-made group appears to have been less hindered by lack of inheritance than those in the other groups. The former industries also allow scope for the entry of small firms with little initial capital. However, this aspect of the problem needs additional evidence and further analysis.

Table 6.4 Estates of Fathers of Top Male Wealth Leavers by Sons' Occupation (constant prices)

	SIC	Over £1,000,000	Over £500,000	Over £250,000	Over £100,000	Over £50,000	Over £25,000	Over £10,000	Over £5,000	Over £1,000	All	Sample Size
				Father's Estate Size: cumulative percentages								
Agriculture	I	14*	27*	41*	58	72*	79*	86*	89*	91*	100	84
Mining	II	8	8	25	50	50	67	67	67	75	100	12
Food	III	13	31*	34	53	63	69	81	81	88	100	32
Chemicals	IV	9	9	17	35	48	52	61	61*	78	100	23
Metal manufacture	V	0	0	46	55	82	82	91	91	91	100	11
Engineering	VI	0	7	15*	34	61	68	73	76	85	100	41
Metal goods n.e.s.	IX	0	0	0*	18*	36	36*	36*	55	64	100	11
Textiles	X	9	25	34	47	66	75	81	85	88	100	32
Clothing	XII	0	7	13	33	47	60	60	60	87	100	15
Paper printing	XV	11	11	42	42	47	58	58	58*	63*	100	19
Construction	XVII	0	0*	5*	23*	32*	32*	50*	55*	68*	100	22
Transport	XIX	5	11	26	53	58	58	69	74	74	100	19
Distribution	XX	4	13	32	59*	71*	76	85*	85	89	100	95
Finance	XXI	10	17	22	35*	46*	53*	67	74	78	100	91
Professions	XXII	8	21	35	51	65	79*	84	91*	94*	100	80
Miscellaneous services	XXIII	0	5	11	26*	37*	37*	53*	53*	69	100	19
Public administration	XXIV	25*	42*	58*	88*	88*	88*	92*	92	92	100	24
Multiple interests	XXV	10	24	38	50	62	64	72	76	84	100	50
All SICs		8	17	30	48	59	66	75	78	84	100	734

* Statistically significantly different at the 5 per cent level from total sample data.

Table 6.5   *Estates of Fathers of Top Male Wealth Leavers, Self-Made and Inheritor Occupational Groups (constant prices)*

Son's SIC	Father's Estate Size: cumulative percentages										
	Over £1,000,000	Over £500,000	Over £250,000	Over £100,000	Over £50,000	Over £25,000	Over £10,000	Over £5,000	Over £1,000	All	Sample Size
ASSOCIATED WITH SELF-MADE Chemicals IV, Metal goods n.e.s. IX, Clothing XII, Paper printing XV, Construction XVII, Transport XIX, Finance XXI, Miscellaneous services XXIII	6	11*	19*	34*	45*	50*	61*	65*	74*	100	219
ASSOCIATED WITH INHERITORS Agriculture I, Food III, Metal manufacture V, Textiles X, Distribution XX, Professions XXII, Public administration XXIV	10*	22*	37*	57*	70*	77*	85*	83*	90*	100	358
All	8	17	30	48	59	66	75	78	84	100	734

* Statistically significantly different at the 5 per cent level from total sample data and between categories of inheritor and self-made SICs.

Fathers' Occupations

An analysis of the occupations of the fathers of top wealth leavers was carried out in much the same way as that for sons, described in the previous section. The results depicted in Table 6.6 bear an interesting relationship to those of Table 6.4. They show a distinct similarity in some of the occupations favouring inherited and self-made wealth and an equally remarkable contrast in others. Agriculture and Metal manufacture remain industry groupings where inherited wealth appears to predominate whether fathers' or sons' SIC is employed. Similarly, Construction and Metal goods n.e.s. favour the self-made for both generations. However, there are pronounced differences dependent on whether fathers' or son's occupational classification is used as the basis of classification. The most remarkable are perhaps that while sons in public administration and the professions were outstandingly those with inherited wealth, fathers in these two groups appear to have favoured rather the self-made. Not too much should be made of the last finding. The SIC groupings are very broad and include wide ranges of different skill and prestige jobs in the same Order, e.g. a postman and the head of the Home Civil Service would both be allocated to Order XXIV.

Father–Son Occupational Mobility and SICs

The existence of such a similarity in the father–son occupation data suggested that a further procedure might be followed in which each son is classified according to whether his stated occupation was the same as that of his father and then to examine the relative importance of inheritance for this group. The results of this analysis are shown in Table 6.7(a) and show that those sons following in their fathers' footsteps were much more closely associated with inherited wealth: 80 per cent were preceded by fathers leaving estates in excess of £25,000, compared with 56 per cent of those who changed occupations.

Table 6.7(b) shows, however, that when the comparison is restricted to sons preceded by *rich* fathers, the relationship is a good deal weaker and not statistically significant. Although more sons in the sample tended to follow the same occupations as their fathers (54 per cent) than for the population data as a whole (44 per cent), the relationship between sons' wealth and fathers' estate size is stronger for sons following fathers' occupations but only slightly so. Whether there is a tendency for sons of rich fathers to leave larger estates if they follow their fathers' occupation is shown differently in Table 6.7(c). Here the data of the two forward tracing samples are employed and the table shows the size of sons' estates according to the father–son occupation distinction for those sons of the super-rich dying in 1902 and 1924–6. Here there is a clearer trend towards larger estates left by sons with the same occupation as their father. The finding illustrates perhaps a (quite understandable) tendency for fathers to favour in their wills sons who carry on the same occupation.

A different approach to the subject of occupational mobility among the wealthy is via the identification of SIC groups where there are

Table 6.6 Estates of Fathers of Top Male Wealth Leavers by Fathers' Occupation (constant prices)

Father's SIC		Father's Estate Size: cumulative percentages									Sample Size
	Over £1,000,000	Over £500,000	Over £250,000	Over £100,000	Over £50,000	Over £25,000	Over £10,000	Over £5,000	Over £1,000	All	
Agriculture I	9	25*	37	55	64	73	85*	88*	89	100	106
Mining II	0	15	39	62	69	77	85	92	92	100	13
Food III	22*	41*	43	59	70	73	78	81	89	100	37
Chemicals IV	13	13	25	56	75	81	81	88	94	100	16
Metal manufacture V	0	8	67*	75	83	83	83	83	83	100	12
Engineering VI	0	7	13*	30*	57	57	67	67	84	100	30
Metal goods n.e.s. IX	9	9	18	36	55	64	73	73	82	100	11
Textiles X	15	24	38	47	71	79	85	85	91	100	34
Clothing XII	0	15	23	54	69	77	77	77	85	100	13
Timber XIV	0	10	20	20	20*	20*	50	50*	70	100	10
Paper printing XV	11	11	39	50	67	72	78	78	84	100	18
Construction XVII	0	0*	4*	29	38*	46*	58*	63	75	100	24
Transport XIX	8	11	24	46	54	54	70	70	76	100	37
Distribution XX	4	14	30	51	61	68	74	77	82	100	139
Finance XXI	13	26	36	53	72	81*	85	89	92	100	47
Professions XXII	5	8*	16*	33*	49	60	73	79	86	100	77
Miscellaneous services XXIII	0	8	8	17*	17*	17*	25*	42*	58*	100	12
Public administration XXIV	7	13	27	37	47	53	60*	67	74	100	30
Multiple interests XXV	23*	39*	52*	68*	68	71	71	77	77	100	31
All SICs	8	17	30	48	59	66	75	78	84	100	734

* Statistically significantly different at the 5 per cent level from total sample data.

Table 6.7   Estates of Fathers of Top Male Wealth Leavers Having the Same or Different Occupations as their Fathers (constant prices)

Father/Son Occupation	Father's Estate Size: cumulative percentages										Sample Size
	Over £1,000,000	Over £500,000	Over £250,000	Over £100,000	Over £50,000	Over £25,000	Over £10,000	Over £5,000	Over £1,000	All	
(a) All Top Wealth Leavers											
Different	7	15	23*	38*	49*	56*	64*	69*	76*	100	390
Same	9	20	38*	59*	72*	80*	88*	90*	94*	100	324
All estates	8	17	30	48	59	66	75	88	84	100	734
(b) Top Wealth Leavers preceded by rich fathers											
Different	13	27	42	68	88	100	100	100	100	100	218
Same	11	25	47	74	90	100	100	100	100	100	258
All estates	12	26	45	72	89	100	100	100	100	100	476
(c) Son's estate size and occupation in forward tracing samples of sons of rich males dying in 1902 and 1924–6											
Different	4	8	21	40*	54*	73*	86	94	96	100	148
Same	5	13	30*	56*	78*	89*	94	97	99	100	82
All estates	4	10	25	46	62	79	89	95	97	100	230

* Statistically significantly different at the 5 per cent level from total sample data.

relatively high and low proportions of sons remaining in the same classification as their fathers. Table 6.8 has therefore been prepared with this aim. It is restricted to data about sons with rich fathers – i.e. who left estates in excess of £25,000 in constant prices. It shows that the industries where the highest proportions of inheritors stayed in the same line of business as their fathers were Transport, Clothing, Distribution and Chemicals. The lowest proportions were in Public administration, the Professions, Engineering and Finance.

Table 6.8   *Mobility of Occupational Groups for Fathers of Top Male Wealth Leavers*

	SIC	Per cent sons of rich fathers remaining in father's SIC
Agriculture	I	65
Mining	II	63
Food	III	77
Chemicals	IV	83
Metal manufacture	V	78
Engineering	VI	39
Metal goods n.e.s.	IX	75
Textiles	X	67
Clothing	XII	88
Paper printing	XV	64
Construction	XVII	57
Transport	XIX	100
Distribution	XX	85
Finance	XXI	48
Professions	XXII	36
Miscellaneous services	XXIII	29
Public administration	XXIV	25
Multiple interests	XXV	29
All SICs		58

AGE

The characteristic of wealth leavers about which there is least ambiguity and for which the data is most reliable is their age. That is not to deny profound difficulties in the interpretation of statistics of wealth distribution broken down by age groups, their trend over time and the underlying causes thereof. But there seems at present to be a measure of agreement among authorities that the distribution of wealth within age groups is not very different from the distribution for the population as a whole (Astin, 1975; Atkinson and Harrison, 1978). This is particularly valid for recent years and seems to be due to a trend of increasing wealth of younger men over the present century. A number of possible explanations of this trend suggest themselves, in addition to the overvaluation of life policies at death.[6] One is related to the life cycle hypothesis; another is that the wealth of lower age groups tends to be exaggerated when it is calculated on the basis of the sample of those who die young, simply because there are likely to be higher proportions of such people who die unexpectedly and make, therefore, no provision for dispossessing themselves of their property in order to minimise tax liability.[7] Increasing rates of estate duty over the century would probably raise the incentive to do this for all those with dependents.[8]

A hypothesis could be proposed that there is a differential age effect according to whether wealth was inherited or self-made. If inheritors take possession of their fortunes on average at an earlier age than those with self-made wealth, then premature unexpected death will catch a higher proportion of the former than of the latter. This is not perhaps too unreasonable an assumption, given that the accumulation of large amounts of property from small beginnings takes many years in most cases. The tendency for rich fathers to make *inter vivos* gifts to their sons earlier and earlier as death duties rise, reinforces the argument.

Sons' Age and Inheritance
It is possible to put this hypothesis to a rather crude test with the aid of the data collected in this study. Table 6.9 has been prepared for this purpose.[9] The table shows the relationship between sons' age and fathers' estate size for all backward tracing samples pooled. Table 6.9(a) includes all top wealth leavers and 6.9(b) medium wealth leavers. The question arises of the best age group to select in order to try to test the hypothesis of the previous paragraph. Wedgwood actually argued that inequality in the age group 55–64 might provide a fair guide to the degree of inequality of inherited wealth. He was however writing at a time when death taxes were substantially lower and the catchment periods for gifts *inter vivos* was only three years. A lower maximum age would therefore suggest itself for the postwar period at any rate. Focusing attention therefore on the rows in the tables relating to men dying below the age of 55, one may observe the extent to which they were preceded by rich fathers relative to the population as a whole.

It can be seen from Table 6.9(a) that for top wealth leavers under 55 the importance of fathers' wealth in each estate size class is clearly greater than that for the population as a whole. This picture is also true, if perhaps to a smaller extent, as can be seen in part (b) of the table for medium wealth leavers.

Fathers' Age and Estate Size
The relationship between wealth of fathers and sons classified according to fathers' age at death is tabulated in Table 6.10. In contrast with the tabulations by sons' age at death they tend to show rather a reverse picture, with older fathers being relatively more commonly associated with sons having inherited wealth. As far as top male wealth leavers are concerned there seems little doubt that this is the case. The proportions of sons preceded by fathers leaving over £25,000, for example, for

Table 6.9   Estates of Fathers of Top and Medium Male Wealth Leavers by Sons' Age (constant prices)

Son's Age	Father's Estate Size: cumulative percentages										Sample Size
	Over £1,000,000	Over £500,000	Over £250,000	Over £100,000	Over £50,000	Over £25,000	Over £10,000	Over £5,000	Over £1,000	All	
(a) 'Top' male wealth leavers											
Under 55	11	19	36	53	72	81*	83	83	89	100	36
55–64	6	14	29	49	60	71	77	81	88	100	84
65–69	10	19	29	46	60	63	72	74	76*	100	79
70–74	7	16	29	42	55	63	75	77	82	100	110
75–79	8	18	29	50	59	64	71	74	80	100	147
80 and over	8	18	30	49	60	67	75	80	87	100	276
All estates	8	17	30	48	59	66	75	78	84	100	734
(b) 'Medium' male wealth leavers											
Under 55	0	0	0	20	40	50	70	80	90	100	10
55–64	0	0	3	31	38	52	59	69	79	100	29
65–69	0	0	8	15	46	54	62	69	77	100	13
70–74	0	4	4	31	35	35	46	65	84	100	26
75–79	0	9*	14	29	34	49	66	69	80	100	35
80 and over	1	3	18*	26	36	47	62	66	81	100	73
All estates	1	3	11	27	37	47	60	68	81	100	189

* Statistically significantly different at the 5 per cent level from total sample data.

fathers aged over 80 are greater than is the case for the population as a whole. At the same time the proportions preceded by rich fathers in the lowest age group, under 55, is universally lower than for the full sample of decedents. This could perhaps be due to the fact that fathers accumulate more wealth for sons to inherit the longer they live, though it is not possible to test this hypothesis with the data at present available. It must also be added that these observations do not apply nearly as strongly to the sample of medium wealth leavers, shown in Table 6.10(b).

NOTES

1 The analysis considers the characteristics separately. Partial correlations obtained through multivariate analysis are not considered here.

2 The division between the areas depends mainly upon where the deceased was domiciled but not where the property was located.

3 It has been suggested that the greater inequality discovered in Scotland is attributable to different patterns of owner occupation of housing between the two areas – a factor which would not be expected to affect top wealth groups (Harrison, 1975).

4 There was a decline in the proportion of persons listed in the five directories between 1956–7 and 1973, from about a third to a fifth of the samples. Several possible explanations of this phenomenon suggest themselves. None were able to be tested.

5 It should be added that all tests were re-run using the stricter form of the t-test for differences in proportions. The same cells were found to be statistically significant as in the textual tables based on the simpler formula.

6 This is largely a consequence of inflated (sums assured) insurance values at death. See Atkinson and Harrison (1978), p. 252.

7 In addition there are increased problems of sampling in the young age groups.

8 The substitution of CTT for estate duty is not relevant here because the data refer to no later than 1973.

9 It has recently been shown that the great bulk of bequests through wills go to people who are themselves already in middle or old age. The numbers of estates available for testing the hypothesis is therefore understandably low. (Diamond Commission, 1977, ch. 8, para. 400, p. 188.)

Table 6.10 Estates of Fathers of Top and Medium Male Wealth Leavers by Fathers' Age (constant prices)

Father's Age	Father's Estate Size: cumulative percentages										Sample Size
	Over £1,000,000	Over £500,000	Over £250,000	Over £100,000	Over £50,000	Over £25,000	Over £10,000	Over £5,000	Over £1,000	All	
(a) 'Top' male wealth leavers											
Under 55	6	10*	18*	30*	40*	46*	62*	63*	76*	100	99
55–64	6	15	27	44	62	71	76	81	91	100	104
65–69	12	29*	38	55	62	71	79	86	90	100	89
70–74	6	12	25	47	60	66	77	81	85	100	109
75–79	11	20	44*	65*	74*	80*	86*	89*	91	100	117
80 and over	9	23	33	53	69	77	86*	89*	93*	100	142
All estates	8	17	30	48	59	66	75	78	84	100	734
(b) 'Medium' male wealth leavers											
Under 55	0	7	15	22	33	41	56	56	81	100	27
55–64	0	0	9	13	22	35	56	69	82	100	23
65–69	0	0	4	22	39	43	56	61	78	100	23
70–74	3	7	21	41	45	62	69	79	86	100	29
75–79	0	0	7	26	41	44	70	70	74	100	27
80 and over	0	3	10	35	38	53	63	78	98*	100	40
All estates	1	3	11	26	36	46	62	70	83	100	189

* Differences in proportions statistically significantly different at the 5 per cent level from total sample data.

7

The Contribution of Inheritance to the Perpetuation of Wealth Inequality

And to leave what with his toil he won
To that unfeather'd two-legged thing, a son.
John Dryden, *Absalom and Achitophel*

This chapter attempts to assess the extent to which inequalities in the distribution of wealth can be explained by inheritance. The data so far have been presented as tabulations of the association between various levels of individuals' personal wealth and that of their predecessors and successors. The present analysis goes further and tries to draw conclusions, albeit tentatively, about the contribution which inheritance makes to the overall distribution of wealth. There are tremendous practical and theoretical problems in such an attempt: in the data at our disposal, in the lack of any accepted model of the accumulation and transmission of personal wealth, and in any attempt to disentangle inheritance as a separate contributory factory from the mass of other interacting influences.

GALTON'S TECHNIQUE

The technique which will be applied is based on Galton's path, breaking work on the relationship between the heights of fathers and their sons – a particular example of an inherited characteristic – in which he introduced the idea of 'regression towards the mean'. Galton (1892) noted that 'If children *on average*, resemble their parents, giants become more gigantic and dwarfs more dwarfish. The tendency of regression towards the mean is that the filial centre is not the parental centre but closer to mediocrity.' Applied to the topic of inherited wealth this means that one must expect to find that a son of a very wealthy father is also wealthy but not quite as wealthy as his father. If that were not so, wealth would become ever more unequally distributed as time proceeds. In Chapter 3 it was shown that two-thirds of the sons whose fathers died rich in 1902 and 1924–6 could be classed as dissipators. What is now required is a method of quantifying precisely how much less wealthy sons are than their fathers. This is summarised in the regression coefficient (β).

The other element which is required in addition is the variance of self-made wealth. This is the proportion of the total variance in wealth which is not explained by the part due to inheritance.

Data used in this chapter are confined to the five samples for which father–son wealth data have been collected. This is simply because the data relating to the wealth of women and of other relatives is not available in sufficient detail to be used in the way about to be described..

These samples were described earlier but one particularly important feature needs to be recalled here because of its special relevance. Some of the samples (called 'backward tracing') were based on rich *sons*, for which the wealth of fathers were traced. Other samples (called 'forward tracing') were based on rich *fathers* whose sons' wealth was then traced. The former kind of samples are those of 1973, 1965 and 1956–7. The latter are those of 1924–6 and 1902. All estate values are expressed at constant 1956–7 prices.

METHOD

The analytical technique used here will be illustrated in detail by taking one of these samples, working through the method of analysis and examining the significance of the results obtained.

Consider then the relationship between fathers' and sons' wealth in the sample drawn for the year 1902. It will be recalled that the relationship between sons' assumed inheritances[1] and the size of their own estates led to a division between so-called accumulators and dissipators. This data included in Table 3.7 is reproduced in Table 7.1 for convenience. The columns show the size of sons' inheritances and the rows the cumulative percentages of sons leaving estates of varying size. Thus, for example, in the first inheritance size class over £250,000, 35 per cent of sons left at least as much as this. Similarly, in the inheritance size class of £100,000 to £250,000, 12 per cent are classed as accumulators (leaving more than £250,000), 26 per cent left estates minimally in their own inheritance range and the remaining 74 per cent were therefore dissipators.

Table 7.1   *Estates of Sons and Fathers Dying in 1902 (constant prices)*

Son's 'Inheritance'	*Son's Estate Size: cumulative percentages*					
	Over £250,000	Over £100,000	Over £50,000	Over £25,000	All	Sample Size
Over £250,000	35	57	68	88	100	101
£100,000 and under £250,000	12	26	52	64	100	50
£50,000 and under £100,000	5	32	42	58	100	19
All over £50,000	25	45	61	78	100	170

Note: Son's inheritance is father's estate size divided by the number of his sons.

It may be added that the median intergeneration span between the dates of death of fathers and sons in the 1902 sample was 32 years. Hence the median year of sons' death is 1934. The object of the exercise is to separate the influences of inheritance from all other factors, including chance and the opportunity to become self-made, in determining the distribution of wealth in 1934[2] by reference to the pattern of inheritance from fathers in 1902, and the accumulation and dissipation of wealth by their sons. In other words, the measured inequality in 1934 is to be attributed in part to the inherited inequality from 1902 and the residual part to the inequality of self-made wealth.[3]

If the distribution of wealth fits the log normal with a satisfactory degree of approximation[4] it is possible to use the variances of the logarithm of wealth in the years 1902 and 1934 as summary measures of inequality. It is concomitant and consistent with that approach to measure the degree of regression towards the mean by taking ordinary least squares estimates of the relationship between fathers' and sons' wealth after transforming the data to logarithms.

During the period ending in 1934 there was a substantial decline in the degree of inequality, in that the share of the top 1 per cent of wealth holders fell from 70 per cent in 1911–13 to 55 per cent of personal wealth (Daniels and Campion, 1936; Atkinson and Harrison, 1978). Similarly, the share of the top 10 per cent of wealth holders fell from 92 to 86 per cent of personal wealth. In terms of the standard deviation of the logarithms there was a decline from 2·85 to 2·46.[5]

The relationship between the wealth of fathers and of their sons for the period was estimated as follows:

$$\log w_s = \alpha + \beta \log w_f + \log u \qquad \qquad \ldots (1)$$

where $\log w_s$ is the logarithm of sons' wealth
                  $\log w$ is that of fathers' wealth
and $\log u$ is the logarithm of the residual.

The size of the coefficient β shows the strength of the regression element. The tendency for regression towards the mean is stronger the more the value of β falls below unity. The standard deviation of the logarithm of the residual (denoted below by σu) represents the influence of 'chance' elements on those individuals leading to self-made wealth. According to the formulation the chance elements act *multiplicatively* in determining son's wealth; hence the son's wealth consists of the *product* of the father's wealth that he inherited and the effects of regression and chance.

THE CONTRIBUTION OF INHERITANCE 1902–34

The statistical estimation of equation (1) was as follows:

$$\log w_s = 2 \cdot 48 + 0 \cdot 46 \log w_f + u$$
$$(0 \cdot 15)$$

The value of 0·46 indicates the strong regression tendencies.[6] For example, fathers who left £1,000,000 would be expected to have sons with a medium wealth of about £180,000, though around this value there would be an extensive spread because of the large standard error.

The next step is to estimate the contribution which the value of the regressive tendency of the association between fathers' and sons' wealth, together with the estimate of the degree of inequality in 1902, make to inequality in 1934.

This can be expressed as follows:

$$\sigma^2_s = b^2_{sf}\, \sigma^2_f + \sigma^2_u \qquad \qquad \dots (2)$$

where σ^2_s is the variance of the logs of the distribution of wealth of sons in 1934

         σ^2_f is the variance of the logs of the distribution of wealth of fathers in 1902

         σ^2_u is the variance of the logs of the residual

and b_{sf} is the coefficient of regression tendencies.

The relationship combines what is known from the *sample* data (b_{sf}) with that which is known about inequality in the *population* distribution at these two points in time. Thus the variance in the distribution of wealth represented by σ^2_s is decomposed into that element which is due to inherited factors ($b^2_{sf}\,\sigma^2_f$) and that due to chance factors (σ^2_u) (the inequalities of natural ability, of the environment etc.), which stands here for 'self-made' wealth.

Substituting values into this equation (2) yield the following results:

$$(2·46)^2 = (0·46^2)\,(2·85^2) + \sigma^2_u$$

$$6·05 \;\; = 1·72 + 4.33$$

or in percentage terms $100\% = 28\% + 72\%$

In other words, 28 per cent of the variance of wealth in 1934 may be attributed to inheritance and 72 per cent to chance factors.[7,8]

THE RESULTS FOR OTHER PERIODS

It remains to compare this result for the first period (1902–34) with those for other years. However, because the nature of the sample data in later years is different, one additional step needs to be taken. Equation (1) could be estimated directly for 1902 and 1924–6, because they were both 'forward tracing' samples – starting with a set of rich fathers and then tracing the wealth of their sons. Sons' estates could then take any value in relation to fixed values of each father's estate – in this case fathers who left more than £100,000 in 1902 prices.

The samples for more recent periods on the other hand were 'backward tracing', the starting point for which was a sample of rich sons whose fathers were then traced. In terms of sample design, fathers' estates effectively become (in statistical terms) the dependent variable. Such data would normally yield biased estimates of equation (1), the relationship between sons' and fathers' wealth.[9] All sons are wealthy by definition because of the sampling frame, whereas fathers may be rich or poor. However, an unbiased estimate of the regression equation can be obtained by using textbook formulae on certain assumptions. The details of the method are relegated to Appendix D.

The methods outlined above were used to evaluate the contributions made by inheritance and chance reflected in the six samples of the father–son wealth relationship drawn over the seventy-year period between 1902 and 1973. The value of b lay between 0·35 and 0·61, suggesting that there was throughout a strong tendency for regression towards the mean.

Table 7.2 shows the results of using equation (2) to partition inequality due to inheritance on the one hand and to self-made factors on the other. The first of the two dates given in the table is the year in which each sample was drawn. The second date is that of the median year of either sons' death (forward tracing samples) or of fathers' death (backward tracing samples).

Table 7.2   *The Influence of Inheritance and Self-Made Factors in the Distribution of Wealth*

	σ_s^2		$b_{sf}^2 \sigma_f^2$		σ_u^2
(a) Forward Tracing Samples					
1902 – 1934	6·05	=	1·72	+	4·33
	100%	=	28%		72%
1924–6 – 1956–7	4·75	=	1·72	+	3·03
	100%	=	36%		64%
(b) Backward Tracing Samples					
1956–7 – 1916	4·75	=	1·51	+	3·24
	100%	=	32%		68%
1965–1928	3.57	=	1·59	+	1·98
	100%	=	45%		55%
1973–1936	3·03	=	2·04	+	0.99
	100%	=	67%		33%

The trends lying behind the figures in Table 7.2 are more directly shown if the samples are re-ordered to reflect chronologically the initial year of the periods they cover. This is done in Table 7.3. Broadly speaking the tables show a tendency for inheritance to explain an increasing (and self-made factors therefore a decreasing) proportion of the subsequent inequality in wealth distribution over the period. In interpreting these results it is important to remember that wealth inequality (as measured both by the variance and by the share of the top percentiles) has declined since the beginning of the century, as shown in Table 7.4.

Table 7.3 *Proportionate Influence of Inheritance and Self-Made Wealth, 1902–73*

Sample Period	Inheritance %	Self-Made Wealth %
1902 – 1934	28	72
1916–1956–7	32	68
1924–6 – 1956–7	36	64
1928 – 1965	45	55
1936 – 1973	67	33

Table 7.4 *Trends in the Variance of Wealth at Median Fathers' and Sons' Dates of Death*

Sample Period	σ_f^2	σ_s^2
1902 – 1934	8·12	6·05
1916 – 1956–7	8·12	4·75
1924–6 – 1956–7	6·71	4·75
1928 – 1965	6·30	3·57
1936 – 1973	5·95	3·03

It can be seen from the table that the decline of 5 points in the variance (from 8·12 to 3·03 in the period 1902–73) is almost all attributable to the decline in the self-made component (σ_u^2 shown in Table 7.5), which declined by 3 points from 4·30 to 0·99. The contribution of inheritance in *absolute* terms is in contrast almost unchanged at 1·72 and 2·04 at the beginning and end of the period (see Table 7.2).

Table 7.5 *Trends in the Importance of 'Self-Made' Wealth Over the Period 1902–73*

Sample Period	σ_u^2
1902 – 1934	4·33
1916 – 1956–7	3·24
1924–6 – 1956–7	3·03
1928 – 1965	1·98
1936 – 1973	0·99

In the early period the residual scatter, as exemplified by Table 7.5, is much greater than for later periods. Thus, as time passed relatively fewer sons would change position in the wealth distribution, despite the fact that the regression tendencies in society did not change very greatly over the period (see Table 7.6 below). This may provide some measure of the increasing lack of opportunity to change positions in the distribution of wealth in later periods.

CONFIDENCE LIMITS

In order to know how much confidence to put in the results tabulated above it is necessary to examine the standard error of the b coefficient (the measure of the regression tendency) and this is shown in Table 7.6. The standard error of the regression coefficient is a measure of the degree to which the regression line can be expected to 'wobble', within confidence limits. In the early period the b coefficient could, on the usual confidence interval, be as high as 0·75. This could in the extreme case increase the importance of inheritance as a contribution to inequality from 28 per cent as shown in Table 7.2, to as much as 76 per cent. Extending the argument to the results for all periods it is clear that, whereas the trend shown by the sample values seems reasonably consistent, the results of any one sample estimate cannot be relied upon. In order to obtain more reliable estimates the data in combinations of adjacent samples were pooled experimentally.

Table 7.6   *The Reliability of the Estimates*

Sample Period	b_{sf}	SE(b)
1902 – 1934	0·46	0·15
1924–6 – 1956–7	0·51	0·28
1916 – 1956–7	0·35	0·15
1928 – 1965	0·36	0·30
1936 – 1973	0·59	0·07

In the event the fit was improved by combining the two forward tracing samples and by pooling those of 1956–7 and 1965. The estimated b coefficients are both then 0·48, with reduced standard errors of 0·13 and 0·09 respectively. The contribution of inheritance becomes 31 per cent for the early and 40 per cent for the late period.

EXPLANATIONS

There is no shortage of possible explanations of the results presented above. They depend on the acceptability of assumptions underlying the model, the data itself and appreciation of the historical process.

The reduction in the variance of the logarithm of the self-made factors, from 4·30 to 0·99 over the period, may reflect both a lower embarkation on risky projects and a greater stability in the economic environment in the postwar period. Both are conducive to the perpetuation of inheritances and inequality. It is, however, necessary to view the results of this chapter which indicates increasing importance of inheritance in the light of those of Chapter 3 which showed a tendency for the proportions of men with rich fathers to fall between the 1950s and the 1970s.

Separation by Sons' Estate Size
Several explanations of the differing conclusions are possible. One might

be related to a particular kind of sampling bias. There is some reason to doubt whether it is justifiable to estimate the regression coefficient for entire distributions from data collected mainly from the top end. Such a procedure would be inappropriate, for example, if tax avoidance practices, affecting observed probate values of estates, were relatively more indulged in by the rich.

Some light may be thrown on this if the data for 1973 are separated into two classes of sons' wealth holding – those of smaller to medium sized estates of up to £100,000 and estates of over £100,000. Table 7.7 decomposes the estimates for this year into two parts.

Table 7.7   *Influence of Inheritance and Self-Made Wealth, Large and Small Estates, 1973*

			Decomposition		
1973	b_{sf}	σ_s^2	$=$ $b_{sf}^2 \sigma_f^2$	$+$	σ_u^2
Large Estates	0·44	3·03	$=$ 1·17	$+$	1·86
	(0·29)	100%	39%		61%
Smaller Estates	0·56	3·03	$=$ 1·88	$+$	1·15
	(0·11)	100%	62%		38%
Pooled all Estates	0·59	3·03	$=$ 2·04	$+$	0·99
	(0·07)	100%	67%		33%

It can be seen that there is a suggestion that smaller estates in this analysis show a stronger relationship between sons' and fathers' wealth than that which exists among the top wealth leavers, but the difference is not statistically significant. A greater inheritance component for the former small estates is also suggested. When the data are pooled, in comparison, the reliability of the estimate, as well as the inheritance component increases.

However, the disaggregated data still show a greater attribution to inheritance for large estates for 1973 than for previous years. The differential is admittedly less and could be accounted for by the large standard error. Since the regression coefficient for large estates in 1973 is not statistically different from zero, comparisons between the samples for 1973 above and other years cannot be relied on. Nevertheless, the observed trend of Table 7.3 is to an extent impressive and further consideration of the need for its reconciliation with the results of Chapter 3 is called for.

The increased importance of inheritance has to be seen here in the light of the decline that has taken place in the inequality of the wealth distribution. The increasing equality arises principally from the effects of a larger reduction in the variance of wealth due to self-made factors[10] than of that due to inheritance. The increasing equality can itself be the source of explanation and reconciliation of the two apparently opposing results. A graphical explanation of how the proportions of self-made persons might rise over the period while inheritance appears more important is given in Appendix E.

QUALIFICATIONS AND CONCLUSIONS

Before attempting firmer conclusions it is necessary to take account of a number of qualifications which must be made to the analysis of this chapter. These are of two kinds: one related to the nature of the data used to estimate the statistical model, and the other to its specification. Any or all can influence the interpretation of the results.

Data Problems
Many of these are discussed at length in Chapter 2. The following are among those of most relevance here.

(a) The variance of the population wealth distributions are based on data which include both males and females whereas the sample data relate only to males. Since women's wealth distribution is more unequal than is that of men, this means that the population variances overstate the degree of inequality compared with the more appropriate variances of male wealth. To determine the effect of this on the results one needs also to know the relative movements that have taken place over the period in the variances of male as against female wealth. This information is not well documented. However, since the share of women in total wealth has risen fairly substantially over the period one might infer that the *decline* in wealth inequality has probably been understated compared with the relevant statistic. If this is correct the effect on the estimation of the statistical model here would, *ceteris paribus*, be to reinforce the conclusion that inheritance had tended to become more important.

(b) The two 'forward tracing' and the three 'backward tracing' samples have inevitably involved different treatment in the way in which the data have entered into the statistical model. The pairs of observations in the later (backward tracing) samples are simply of each son's wealth and that of his father. On the other hand the earlier forward tracing samples included data about *all* sons and the observations are the average of brothers' wealth and 'inheritance' is defined as father's total wealth divided by the number of his sons. The method of sampling in the former cases almost never included (except when two brothers died in the same year by chance) more than one son.

(c) There is likely to have been a significant stepping up of tax avoidance over the seventy-year period with increasing marginal rates of estate duty. This implies that the observations in the earlier period may more accurately reflect an individual's wealth than those in the later period. However, this may offset the effects of assuming that in the forward tracing samples a father's estate was divided between all his sons, whereas in the samples working backwards the implicit assumption is that a son inherited the whole of his father's estate.

(d) There are variations in the intergeneration spans in the various samples being lower in the early samples, implying a shorter period in which wealth is 'turned over' between generations, and the greater the time period the more the opportunity for both accumulation and dissipation. If the observed differences in intergeneration spans are, at least in part, due to sampling errors, this would tend to lead to biased underestimates of sons' wealth in the later samples and therefore to understatement of the regression coefficient, thus strengthening the overall conclusion of the analysis.

(e) Arising from and related to (d) above, one sample, that of 1924–6, includes a relatively high proportion of sons still living. The father–son wealth data therefore is unrepresentative of the population to the extent that it excludes a number of older sons. Given the rather weak relationship between son's age and inheritance (see Chapter 6) and the fact that such a bias affects only a single sample, it seems fair to regard its influence on the results as minimal.

Problems Relating to the Specifications and Assumptions of the Model

(a) The percentage of the variance of wealth attributed to inheritance is based on the assumption that sons' wealth is log linearly related to fathers' wealth. If some more complex non-linear relation held in reality, the proportion attributed to inheritance could be increased, and the self-made element reduced.

(b) The evidence on inheritance patterns is heavily influenced by samples relating to the top end of the wealth distribution. Extrapolation to the less wealthy would not be justified if different patterns hold lower down in the distribution. Indeed, the differences in the estimates for large and small estates described above for 1973 suggest that extrapolation downwards may not be justified and that either some alternative behaviour is to be expected among small wealth holders (whose wealth might better be explained by a simple life cycle model) or that the incentive for tax avoidance among large wealth holders is such that the statistics are inadequate at the top end of the distribution.

(c) The method of decomposition in terms of variances is not necessarily the only possibility; others include comparisons in terms of standard deviations or gini coefficients.[11]

(d) Finally, and perhaps most importantly, the specification of the model is relatively simple and omits a number of factors which are important in the transmission and concentration of wealth. For example, it excludes the effect of intermarriage among the wealthy, of inheritances from relatives other than fathers, of estate duty and other taxes, of different patterns of legacy and bequests, and so forth.[12]

The directional effects of some of these excluded factors can be little more than surmised. For instance, the effect of multiple inheritances on the results would be to increase the degree of regression towards the mean, but this would tend to be moderated by the increasing importance of trust and *inter vivos* gifts stimulated by high tax rates which would lead to understatement of sons' wealth in later years. If all the other possible effects of data deficiencies are brought into the picture the situation becomes extremely complex and it would be cavalier to offer more than an opinion as to the net overall directional bias of the results presented in this chapter.

There is, thus, clearly much scope for an improved and larger study. The present results have been offered because the method of analysis is thought to provide a different way of looking at the manner whereby inheritance affects inequality. Further, and in the absence of any evidence to the contrary,[13] the trends which appear from the limited samples may well – in broad outline at least – reflect correctly what has been happening in the population at large.

NOTES

1 Defined as fathers' total wealth divided by the number of his sons.
2 The simplification is here made that the distribution of wealth in the median year of death of all sons approximates to the weighted average of the distributions of wealth of all years in which sons in the sample died.
3 Inequality in 1934 therefore depends on the size of the regression coefficient and chance factors. Given a tendency of a regression towards the mean, if chance factors are great this will lead to greater inequality in the following period.
4 We are interested in the contribution of inheritance to the inequality of the whole wealth distribution for which the log normal is broadly adequate. Nevertheless we realise that other approximations may give better fits for the tail.
5 The estimates of the standard deviation are based on the method of quantiles relating to the top 1 per cent. If based on the top 10 per cent of wealth holders the estimates of the standard deviation of the logarithms are 2·69 and 2·36 (thus confirming that the fit to the log normal was not exact though data inaccuracies are possibilities to be borne in mind). The calculations described below have been carried out on both bases, i.e. using estimates of the standard deviation based on the top 1 and 10 percentiles, but no difference of any substance emerged. Data on percentile shares are those of Atkinson and Harrison (1978).
6 It should be noted that least-squares regression estimates are biased downwards if there are measurement errors in the determining variable. The size of the bias depends on the ratio of the variance of the measurement errors to the total variance of the observations in the sample. In our sample the observed values cover a very wide range and we do not believe therefore that this particular source of error is of serious dimensions.
7 The variance of the chance element (the residual variance) is calculated as a residual, namely, as the difference between the variance in the sons' wealth distribution and $b_{sf}^2 \sigma_f^2$. The variance estimated from the sample data is 2·52.
8 It may be noted that the proportion due to inheritance would be equal to R^2 if the analysis was applied to the whole population. But because the data are chosen from one end of the distribution it is necessary to carry out the above more involved analysis.
9 Hence a father's estate could take any value associated with fixed values of a son's estate (in these cases sons who left more than £100,000 in 1956–7 prices).
10 Partly suggested by greater stability and also increasing marginal rates of taxation on income.
11 Davies and Shorrocks (1978) have shown how very sensitive estimates of the contribution of life cycle savings and inheritance are to the explanation of wealth distribution and to the choice of index of inequality chosen.
12 One advantage of the model used here over most others is that inheritance is the estimated variable and is not relegated to the status of a residual factor (see Davies and Shorrocks, 1978).
13 It is of interest that a very recent study by Menchik (1977) of the father–son wealth relationship for a sample of individuals dying in Connecticut produced a coefficient of regression towards the mean of the same broad order of magnitude as that obtained in this study. This is the more impressive when it is realised that Menchik's sample differed in many respects, particularly in that it was largely restricted to a relatively small number of immobile residents of Connecticut, USA.

8

Inheritance and Inequality

The sole equality on earth is death.
                    Philip James Bailey, *A Country Town*

This book has focused attention on the sources of personal fortunes in
Britain this century. Major interest has centred on those persons at the
top end of the wealth distribution. The study covers a period which,
according to the best estimates available, has seen a substantial decline
in the degree of wealth inequality; none the less, wealth is a good deal
more unequally distributed than is income and the top 1 per cent of
wealthy individuals still probably own in excess of a quarter of the
nation's personal fortunes.

Great wealth confers substantial benefits on its owners: most obvious
is that of potential purchasing power over goods and services, but it can
also bestow corporate power through the ownership of stocks and
shares and, on occasion, even political power via control of the
productive assets and employment opportunities of major companies.
The existence of these benefits has long led to interest in the ways in
which wealth is acquired, in particular whether by inheritance or as a
result of man's own efforts. Concern arises also because the opportunities to build up fortunes in the private sector of an economy is likely to
bear some relationship to progress, innovation and economic growth.

This study is not concerned with the desirability of any particular
shape of wealth distribution or of inheritance pattern, nor in this
concluding chapter will the policy issues arising from the research be
discussed. Its purpose is rather to bring together in summary form the
main conclusions of the detailed statistical analyses which were reached
in earlier chapters.

THE NATURE AND RELIABILITY OF THE DATA

Before discussing any results, however, it is necessary to repeat once
more the cautionary statement that the available data used to measure
wealth and inheritance are not ideal. Most of Chapter 2 is devoted to an
account of the various data deficiencies and the ways in which they can
best be handled. It is impossible to summarise them. But the reader is
reminded that inheritance is quantified very largely on the basis of the

probate values of estates left at death by closely related members of succeeding generations of the same family measured at constant prices. To an extent such data are thought to be quite fair proxies for wealth transmissions and, therefore, are not unreasonable to employ in order to observe patterns and trends in inheritance over time. Moreover, while the results are based on samples which total more than one thousand individuals the standard errors of estimates derived from them for the whole population are nevertheless large.

PATTERNS OF INHERITANCE

Discussion has revolved around four central questions:

(1)   What is the relationship between an individual's wealth and that of his/her predecessors?
(2)   To what extent do those who are known to have received substantial inheritances maintain or dissipate their fortunes?
(3)   What characteristics are more commonly associated with inheritors as distinct from the self-made?
(4)   What trends have taken place in the importance of inheritance during the present century?

THE IMPORTANCE OF PREDECESSORS' WEALTH

Estimation of the relative importance of predecessors' wealth has occupied earlier chapters and was based on four separate samples of individuals. Three of the samples were of *rich males* dying in 1956–7, 1965 and 1973. The fourth was a sample of *rich women* dying in 1973. The data were also classified into three size categories of wealth. The first is 'Top Wealth Leavers' – individuals leaving estates in constant (1956–7) prices of £100,000 and more who were all within the top 0·1 per cent of the wealth distribution. The second category is of 'Medium Wealth Leavers' whose estates fell in the wealth bracket £50,000 to £100,000 (at constant prices) and relate to individuals in the top 1 per cent of the wealth distribution. Finally there is a group of 'Small Wealth Leavers' whose estates were valued at between £7,500 and £50,000 (at constant prices) and who were within the top 10 per cent of the wealth distribution.

THE WEALTH OF FATHERS AND SONS (BACKWARD TRACING SAMPLES)

In all three samples of male wealth leavers a clear positive association was observed between sons' wealth and that of fathers i.e. increasing sons' wealth was associated with a greater proportion of fathers who themselves left large estates. For the richest sons very roughly two-thirds were preceded by fathers leaving in excess of £25,000. This figure was the one most commonly adopted throughout the book as the watershed dividing 'rich' from 'poor' fathers. For sons who were medium wealth holders, proportions having fathers with this minimum sized estate ranged between one-third and nearly three-fifths in the three samples of 1973, 1965 and 1956–7. Taken together about four-fifths of all sons in the top and medium wealth brackets were preceded by fathers whose estates were in excess of £1,000.

Interest attaches also to the role of inheritance in the smallest size class of sons' estates for whom fathers' wealth is, expectedly, less important. However, within the group of small wealth holders the importance of fathers' wealth rises steeply as sons' wealth increases. While 38 per cent of sons whose estates were between £7,500 and £10,000 were preceded by fathers whose wealth was in excess of £1,000, in the next highest sons' wealth size classes (of £10,000 to £25,000 and £25,000 to £50,000) the proportions were 60 and 69 per cent. These statistics may also be read in the light of the fact that median wealth in the population at large is estimated to have reached approximately £100 only in 1956–7 (the base year of the wealth data comparisons in this study). Hence the acquisition of even a moderate level of wealth appears strongly dependent upon having a father who is at least well into the top half of the wealth distribution.

INHERITORS VERSUS SELF-MADE AMONG TOP WEALTH LEAVERS

The question of the proportion of top male wealth leavers who are self-made was discussed in Chapter 3 where four separate methods of comparing fathers' and sons' wealth were used. The results showing possible proportions of self-made persons according to various, albeit arbitrary, criteria are set out again in Table 8.1.

The table examines the proportions of self-made persons according to the different measures and criteria explained in the chapter. The top sections (a) and (b) compare the proportions of sons who were preceded by fathers leaving estates in excess of £10,000, £25,000 and £50,000 using three different index numbers to allow for the great changes in prices that occurred over the period. Section (c) examines proportions of sons who would be classified as self-made on the basis of three compound interest growth rates. Section (d) shows proportions of self-made men defined by reference to whether their fathers left estates which placed them in the top 1, 5 or 10 per cent of the distribution of wealth in their year of death.

The table has been designed to show something of the limits within which men could fairly reasonably be defined as self-made. Three minimum values of fathers' estates are used, for example, to identify inheritance and these are rendered comparable in real terms by the use of three separate index numbers.

The figures in the table speak for themselves and no more can be read into them than is implied by acceptance of the alternative definitions of inheritance and self-made wealth used for their calculation. But if one takes the middle values for all the measures, one concludes that between roughly three-fifths and four-fifths of the top wealth leavers of the 1950s,

Table 8.1   *Proportions of Inheritors among Three Samples of Top Wealth Leavers, 1956–7, 1965 and 1973, According to Different Measures and Different Criteria*

Measure	Criterion	Father's Wealth as multiple of minimum wealth of Top 10% (multiple)	1956–7 RPI %	1956–7 API %	1956–7 YPI %	1965 RPI %	1965 API %	1965 YPI %	1973 RPI %	1973 API %	1973 YPI %
(a) Retail Price Index	Father's Estate										
	greater than £10,000		75			77			71		
	greater than £25,000		68			68			58		
	greater than £50,000		63			55			47		
(b) Different Price Indices	Father's Estate										
	greater than £10,000		79	78	77	83	85	71	76	72	70
	greater than £25,000		72	70	70	74	76	59	62	60	59
	greater than £50,000		67	64	62	60	64	46	51	47	49
(c) Compound Interest Growth Rates	Rate of Growth										
	less than 6%			71			70			71	
	less than 5%			69			63			55	
	less than 4%			64			62			53	
(d) Relative Wealth Index	more than that of Top 10%	1		87			91			82	
	5%	3		81			84			79	
	1%	15		71			74			60	

Note: Estates deflated by RPI in (a) apply to the whole of the data in the three samples. Those estates deflated by RPI in (b) only apply to fathers dying since 1900 and are therefore not strictly comparable. RPI is the Retail Price Index, API is the Asset Price Index and YPI is the Yield Price Index.

1960s and 1970s were inheritors and the remainder, self-made. Using the strictest of the three bench-marks, the limits are approximately a half to three-quarters, while on the most lenient criterion they are more like 70 to 90 per cent. The range of extreme values in the table is certainly wide (from 46 to 91 per cent as inheritors), but the range of assumptions, criteria and adjustments is no less so, and it is perhaps remarkable that the variation is not greater. Taking account of all the price indices and different measures adopted it can be said that the great majority suggest that inheritance accounted for between 60 and 80 per cent of the fortunes of these top wealth leavers. It cannot be pretended that the evidence presented here is capable of greater precision, but perhaps it is not too far from the truth that something between two-thirds and four-fifths of those who died rich in the third quarter of the present century owed their wealth to inheritances and the rest to entrepreneurship and luck.

TRENDS IN THE FATHER–SON WEALTH RELATIONSHIP AMONG TOP
AND MEDIUM WEALTH LEAVERS

It has been possible to examine trends in the importance of fathers' wealth among top and medium wealth leavers over a period of approximately seventy years. The earliest study with which comparisons are possible is the one of Wedgwood based on samples of wealthy sons dying in 1924–6. Comparisons of Wedgwood's results with those of the 1956–7 sample showed virtually no change in the importance of fathers' wealth among top and medium male wealth leavers. Between the 1950s and the 1970s, however, the proportions of rich sons having rich fathers tended to decline, some of the differences between the figures for the two years eventually becoming statistically significant.

Conclusions about trends in the importance of inheritance must be seen also in the light of the results using the different approach of Chapter 7 (see below). Additionally, it is necessary to point out that the results may be to an extent statistical rather than real in so far as the data have become less reliable with increasing tax avoidance by rich fathers over the period. It must also be recalled that there has been a decline in family size over the period whereas the data compare the size of sons' estates with that of the 'whole' of each father's estate. This means that father's wealth is a better proxy for son's inheritance in the later years of the period.

WEALTH ACCUMULATION AND DISSIPATION (FORWARD TRACING
SAMPLES)

Drawing samples of top wealth leavers and tracing the estates left by their fathers precludes the selection of poor sons and cannot, therefore, throw direct light on the extent to which inheritors tend to dissipate their fortunes. In order to remedy this deficiency two samples were drawn of rich men dying in 1902 and 1924–6 and the estates left by their sons traced. These were dubbed 'forward tracing' in contrast to the 'backward tracing' samples of 1956–7, 1965 and 1973. Defining accumulation and dissipation according to whether a son left as much or more than his 'inheritance' (calculated as father's estate divided by the number of his sons), the results of pooling the data for the two years showed that about two-thirds were dissipators and one-third accumulators. Furthermore, 5 per cent of the sons in these years achieved compound interest growth rates equal to or greater than 5 per cent.

NON-PATERNAL SOURCES OF INHERITANCE

Data presented in Table 8.1 of the proportions of those rich who might be described as 'with inherited wealth' should on any criterion be interpreted as minima. This was brought out in Chapter 4 which reported on the results of searches made for the wealth of fathers-in-law among those designated as self-made by a watershed of a father's estate of £25,000. The results confirmed that some men did acquire wealth through marriage, but the numbers turned out to be rather less dramatic than might have been anticipated. Of 78 rich sons with poor fathers for whom the estates of fathers-in-law were traced, only about 1 in 7 had fathers-in-law who left more than £25,000 in 1956–7 prices (though well over a third of fathers-in-law left more than £10,000).

The estates of certain other relatives were also traced in the course of the research, some by chance, others systematically. Mothers' wealth was, expectedly, found to be strongly and positively associated with the wealth of fathers. The association between the wealth of grandfathers and grandsons could just conceivably be regarded as evidence in support of generation skipping, though the pattern was neither simple (because all fathers were rich) nor statistically significant.[1] When the values of the estates of all relatives (including fathers) were included in the analysis the importance of inheritance for top wealth leavers as measured by the proportion of predecessors leaving wealth in excess of £25,000 rose from just over two-thirds to nearly three-quarters. Given the fact that systematic searching for all such other relatives was not undertaken, this fraction should still be regarded as a minimum.

WOMEN AND INHERITANCE

In view of women's substantial share in total personal wealth, a separate sample was drawn of 140 top female wealth leavers of 1973 and the estates of their fathers and husbands were traced. Analysis of the results showed that, compared to a similar sample of men, a considerably higher proportion (72 per cent) came from rich families. Moreover, when husbands' wealth was included in the data the vast majority of such women were classified as inheritors (63 per cent of rich widows were preceded additionally by rich husbands). Fathers' wealth was more important among the thirty-two spinsters in the sample – 84 per cent were preceded by rich fathers. No more than 5 per cent of the women in the whole sample could be regarded as self-made in the entrepreneurial sense. Background information obtained from relatives and other sources in fact confirmed that probably fewer than four or five could be properly placed in the self-made category.

INTERMARRIAGE AMONG THE RICH

Much of the existing information on the distribution of wealth and inheritance is based on data relating to individuals rather than to families. It is important to know something about the extent to which men and women from different wealth classes marry each other. Light could be thrown on this matter by examining the relationship between the fortunes of fathers and fathers-in-law of top married wealth leavers in the samples drawn for this study.

The extent to which intermarriage among the rich occurs depends here, as elsewhere, on the wealth size classes used as bench-marks, but it was shown that about three-fifths of top wealth leavers (of either sex) who came from homes where fathers left more than £25,000 married partners whose fathers' wealth was also greater than the same amount.

IDENTIFIABLE CHARACTERISTICS OF WEALTH LEAVERS

Background information on four characteristics: location, status, occupation and age was available on a systematic basis for the majority of individuals in the samples.

Location

The only consistently reliable evidence about location for the persons included in the study was whether or not they lived in Scotland. In view of the fact that wealth appears to be more unequally distributed in Scotland than in England and Wales it was thought important to try to estimate whether there was any difference in the proportions of sons having rich fathers in the two countries. A sample of top Scottish wealth leavers was therefore drawn for the year 1965, the latest for which comparisons could efficiently be made with England and Wales. The results showed that precisely the same percentage (68 per cent) of sons in the two countries were preceded by fathers leaving estates of £25,000 and over, the bench-mark separating inheritors from the self-made. Hence the evidence cannot be said to support an explanation of differences in the degree of inequality between the two countries as stemming from differences in the relative importance of inherited wealth.

Status

Attempts to allocate all fathers and sons in the samples to one or other of the available social class categories had to be abandoned at an early stage because of lack of data. However, there was one employable characteristic on which information was available which was virtually certain to be correlated with status, rather than simply with wealth. This was whether an individual was or was not listed in one or other of the standard directories employed in the search for fathers' names – *Who's Who*, *Burke's Peerage*, *Burke's Landed Gentry*, *Debrett's* and *Kelly's Directory of the Titled, Landed and Official Classes*. Comparisons of the proportions of sons who were mentioned in these volumes who came from rich families with proportions of the whole population of top wealth leavers proved revealing and not entirely expected. While Peers, Landed Gentry and those in *Who's Who* or *Kelly's Directory* universally came from substantially richer families than did the samples as a whole, the same was not true for Knights Bachelor. Indeed there was only one percentage point difference between the proportions of Knights and that for the total of top wealth leavers whose fathers left estates of over £10,000. This presumably says something about the kinds of person on whom knighthoods have been bestowed (the authors are not quite sure what).

Occupation
Information was available about the occupations of about 90 per cent of the individuals in the samples of top wealth leavers. It was used to allocate them into one of the Orders of the Standard Industrial Classification, which was thought to be the most appropriate compromise industrial/occupational classification system available. The strongest conclusion resulting from the analysis of sons' occupations was that rich sons who were classified in the agricultural sector had the highest proportions of fathers leaving large estates. Other industry groups which tended to favour inherited wealth were food, drink and tobacco, metal manufacturing, textiles, distribution, the professions and public administration. Those groups favouring the self-made were chemicals, metal goods n.e.s., clothing, paper and printing, transport, finance and miscellaneous services. Analysis by fathers' occupations produced some similar results, agriculture and metal manufacturing equally favouring inheritors, and construction and metal goods n.e.s., the self-made. But there were also differences: for example, in public administration and the professions, where fathers tended to have self-made sons. About 53 per cent of the top wealth leavers remained in the same occupational group as their fathers. Moreover, a much higher proportion of them (80 per cent) came from families where the estate size was over £25,000 than of those who changed occupational categories (56 per cent). The relationship between sons' wealth and fathers' estate size was, however, much weaker when the comparison was restricted to sons who were preceded by rich fathers.

Age at Death
The ages at death of the individuals in the samples were known with a fair degree of accuracy for all but the relatively few persons whose death entries were not identified because of a combination of poverty and common name. Analysis by son's age was considered useful in throwing light on estate duty avoidance by gifts *inter vivos*. The proportion of sons

dying under the age of 55 who came from wealthy families was found to be decidedly higher than that for the whole population of all top wealth leavers. On the other hand, analysis according to fathers' age at death showed that it was older fathers who were most commonly associated with sons having inherited wealth, possibly, it may be suggested, because paternal longevity carries with it greater time for wealth to be accumulated and then passed on.

GALTONIAN REGRESSION ANALYSIS AND TRENDS IN THE
IMPORTANCE OF INHERITANCE

The bulk of the analysis in this volume has been based on comparisons of the proportions of, mainly rich, sons who were preceded by fathers leaving estates of varying size. In Chapter 7 a different approach was adopted using the technique made famous by Galton by which estimates of the association between the wealth of fathers and sons leads to the partitioning of the causes of wealth inequality into 'inheritance' and 'chance' factors (representing self-made wealth). Using the variance of the logarithms of the distributions as measures of inequality, the results showed a steady and quite substantial increase in the relative importance of inheritance as the explanatory variable since 1900. This result could equally well be viewed as a decline in the importance of chance factors which provide the opportunities for individuals to engage in making their own fortunes. An understanding of the changing fabric of society is the key to identifying the causes of these events, not the model or the statistics themselves.

The presence of very large standard errors, the existence of several important kinds of data deficiencies and problems arising out of the specification and estimation of the model used to obtain the results referred to in the previous paragraph mean that they cannot be regarded as definitive. Moreover, the conclusions derived from the regression analysis must be seen in the light of those of Chapter 3 which showed an opposite tendency, albeit less marked over at least a part of the period. However, the two sets of results are not necessarily inconsistent with each other. Each approach seeks to answer a different question. One relates to the importance of inheritance generally in wealth inequality. The other is concerned with the sources of wealth of the small proportion of persons at the very top of the distribution.

It is important to be clear about this when drawing policy implications from the results presented in this book. If the focus of attention is with the more obvious affluence of the very wealthy, then one should be interested in the numbers of them who come from wealthy families. On the other hand, if one wants to know whether mobility within the whole distribution is adequate or not then the rate of regression towards the mean is the proper measure to look at. Both are important issues, but they are not the same. For technical reasons it is perfectly possible for the Galtonian techniques to show inheritance to be an increasing determinant of inequality in wealth distribution while there is a fall in the proportions of rich sons (leaving more than £100,000) who were preceded by fathers leaving large estates.

WEALTH AND INEQUALITY

This book has been concerned with the quantification of the importance of inheritance in present day society, though it has naturally not been possible to unravel all the complexities that accompany the process of intergenerational wealth transfers.

If judgement must be reserved about *trends* over time, one firm conclusion seems almost unequivocally to stand out. It is that inheritance is the major determinant of wealth inequality. The regression analysis attributed some two-thirds of the inequality in the distribution of wealth in 1973 to inheritance. The proportions of top wealth leavers since the mid-fifties who were preceded by rich fathers was shown on what might be regarded as conservative assumptions to be in excess of 60 per cent. For example, nearly three-quarters had fathers whose fortunes were at least *ten times* higher than the minimum wealth needed to qualify them for inclusion in the top 10 per cent of the wealth distribution. Moreover, since none of these figures takes account of inheritance from persons other than fathers, they must be regarded as minima. The likelihood of being born to a father who was to die rich is extremely low (P = approx. 0·01); therefore it is difficult to avoid the conclusion that inheritance has been the most important single source of wealth inequality in the fairly recent past in twentieth-century Britain.

NOTE

1 The Diamond Commission's sample survey of estates of £15,000 or over showed that less than 5 per cent of bequests went to third or fourth generations. However, in the largest size class (estates over £500,000) the proportion was as high as 13 per cent. (Diamond, 1977, ch. 8, para. 366, p. 176.)

Appendix A

Table A.1 *Distribution of Estates According to Inland Revenue and Probate Valuations, England and Wales, 1973–4 Average*

Numbers of Estates, Gross and Net Values by Sex of Deceased Numbers

	Probate Values				Inland Revenue Values	
	Gross		Net		Net	
Lower limit of capital value	*Male*	*Female*	*Male*	*Female*	*Male*	*Female*
£100,000	752	488	678	453	1,137	832
£200,000	175	77	129	74 ⎫		
£300,000	88	33	77	31 ⎬	429	223
£500,000	56	16	44	16 ⎭		
Total £100,000 and over	1,071	614	928	574	1,566	1,055

Source: Inland Revenue Statistics (1975), Table 102, and figures supplied by the Central Probate Registry.

Appendix B

Table B.1 *Probate Values of Estates left by Marriott's list of Millionaires (current prices)*

	£
Bridgland, Sir Aynsley	321,237
Cohen, John Solomon	194,821
Cohen, Lewis, Lord	130,565
Cotton, Jack	1,176,074
Edgson, Stanley	121,526
Fenston, Felix	12,670,566
Flack, Walter	840,801
Fox, Cecil Louis	282,620
Hammerson, Lewis	121,600
Harris, Harry	419,671
Harrison, Gabriel	303,898
King, Samuel	2,370,740
Leaver, Marcus	373,163
Littman, Joseph	3,212,787
Myers, Sefton	617,371
Neale, Charles	72,314
Samuel, Howard	3,848,222
Sputz, Otto	107,035
Sunley, Bernard	5,204,764
Wates, Norman Edward	703,279
Wingate, Maurice	1,313,613
Winham, Francis	2,654,337

Source: Marriott (1967).
Note: The figures are taken from the Calendars. Subsequent reswearings not entered thereon are excluded. (See p.36 note 17 above.)

Method of Construction of Price Index Numbers

Four series of price indices are used to compare the estates of fathers and sons at constant prices. Three are of the standard type. The fourth is a relative wealth index and is explained below. This appendix describes the sources of data and method of constructing each index, for each of which the average of the years 1956–7 = 100.

THE RETAIL PRICE INDEX (RPI)

This was the price index for consumer goods and services constructed from that of Jeffreys' and Walters' (1956) series from 1870 to 1952, continued into the retail price index of the London and Cambridge Economic Service and thence into the official Department of Employment series.

ASSET PRICE INDEX (API)

The API was the most complex of those used here. The method of construction is basically similar to that of Sandford and Wright (1969). Sub-indices were compiled for a number of groups of assets and used to construct an overall weighted average API. Two distinct problems were therefore encountered. The first was the choice of assets to include in the index. The second was a problem of weighting the sub-indices. The weights to use for any estate should, of course, be decided by its portfolio. However, this information is not available for individual estates in England and Wales and the proxy weights employed were derived from data published by the Inland Revenue relating to the asset structure of all estates broken down by size.

Choice of Assets

Assets were placed into one of four groups following the method of Sandford and Wright. The first group contains 'near cash' assets. They consist of cash, balances at clearing banks, trustee and post office accounts, mortgage loans, ordinary life policies, farming stock, trade assets of individuals, household goods, government securities, preference and debenture shares. The grouping is based on the assumption that all assets included have maintained a fairly constant monetary value, or at least have changed less in monetary value than the other groups. The second group consists of quoted and unquoted ordinary shares. The third group covers realty including land. The final group comprises residential and industrial buildings and miscellaneous property rights.

Measurement of Price Changes

For the first group of items, by assumption, there are no price changes to be accounted for. The price index for the second group is that of industrial ordinary shares. The source over the period is published by the London and Cambridge Economic Service updated from 1970 by the FT Actuaries Index. The index of groups covering land and miscellaneous reality is based on the price of agricultural land values. The sources of data for this index from 1900 to 1956–7 are those of Ward (1958); between 1959 and 1967 those of Peters (1966). Thereafter they are those published by the Inland Revenue.

The index for the last group of assets, from 1900 to 1969, consisting of residential and industrial buildings, is that compiled by the London and Cambridge Economic Service on a sample of existing houses sold with vacant possession. From 1970 the data source is the Nationwide Building Society's index numbers of existing dwellings sold with vacant possession.

Method of Weighting Sub-indices

The final step in the construction of the index was to obtain data on the asset structure of individual estates over the period 1900–73 to use as weights for the four sub-indices.

Data on the asset composition of estates by size class were obtained from the Inland Revenue Reports and Statistics. Choice of years was restricted by those in which the IR published the full information. It was felt that the statistics for nine separate years to cover the proportions of assets in various estate size classes would be adequate for the purpose. These were 1905, 1914, 1925, 1935, 1938, 1949, 1956, 1965, 1973. The last three years were chosen to cover those in which the samples of sons were drawn in order that they could be adjusted to 1956–7 prices.

The size classes chosen to break down the asset composition of estates varied over the period in the Inland Revenue Reports and Statistics and the wealth size brackets used for the analysis were as follows:

(1)   less than £20,000
(2)   £20,000 and under £50,000
(3)   £50,000 and under £100,000
(4)   £100,000 and under £500,000 and
(5)   £500,000 and over.

THE YIELD PRICE INDEX (YPI)

The YPI is based on the yield on consols for the period 1900–73. The yields were then adjusted for changes in the prices of consumer goods and services using the RPI. The data are based upon those published by the London and Cambridge Economic Service for 1900 to 1970; later years were available from the Annual Abstract of Statistics published by the Central Statistics Office.

It is hardly necessary to add that the indices constructed are in no sense ideal. However, they provide approximations to changes in prices over the period. Being, moreover, quite different in conception the three indices together can be said to test something of the sensitivity of the main results to different measures of price changes.

RELATIVE WEALTH INDEX (RWI)

The RWI was constructed in order to obtain a series by which the wealth of a father at his death may be compared with that of the distribution of wealth obtaining in that year. The index can then be used to hold constant an estate of a given size in the size distribution of personal wealth so as to ascertain the proportions of a group of wealth holders whose fathers had occupied different positions in the distribution.

The first step was to decide on the bench-mark against which the wealth of any given father might be compared. This could in principle be one of the measures of central tendency such as the mean or median wealth, but the greater interest in the proportions of the wealthy with antecedents in the highest wealth groups implied that a more appropriate bench-mark would be the minimum wealth needed for inclusion in the top 1, 5 or 10 per cent of the distribution in any particular year.

Estimating the Minimum Money Value of Wealth of the Top 10 Per Cent

The minimum wealth of the top 10 per cent was not directly observable from any statistical source. The data available for most years in the period were:

(a) the total of personal wealth and
(b) the percentage share in personal wealth of the top 10 per cent.

In order to find the minimum wealth of the top 10 per cent it was necessary to estimate, first mean adult population wealth (m) which could easily be derived from (a) above. The second step involved making an assumption of the shape of the wealth distribution itself which was that it approximated the log normal.[1] Using the method of Prais (1976) it is then possible to estimate the standard deviation from data on population shares in personal wealth.

Given m, and σ the minimum wealth of the top 10 per cent may then be estimated as follows:

$$\log w_{\min 10\%} = \mu + 1{\cdot}282\sigma$$

where $\log w_{\min 10\%}$ is the logarithm of the required minimum
$\qquad\qquad \mu$ $\qquad\quad$ is the log of median wealth
and $\qquad 1{\cdot}282\sigma$ $\qquad$ is the size of the standard deviation

which is added (in logs) to the median to give a level of wealth above which all persons holding that wealth are in the top 10 per cent of the wealth distribution. When only mean wealth m and σ are known the median μ may be obtained from the following relationship:

$$\mu = me^{-\frac{1}{2}\sigma^2}$$

Tables using this formula which provide the ratio of the mean to the median are given in Aitchison and Brown (1957).

Data Available

The data on total wealth and the percentage share of the top 10 per cent in England and Wales used in the estimates are those provided by Atkinson and Harrison (1978). These data do not, however, cover all the years between 1900 and 1973. The series starts only in 1923 and there are certain gaps, namely 1931–5, 1937, 1939–49 and 1963. The data on wealth shares are also deficient for our purposes because for a number of years the share of the top 10 per cent is not given though those of the top 1 and 5 per cent are.[2]

Figures for missing years between 1923 and 1973 were graphically interpolated on the basis of a three-year moving average and assuming linearity from derived data on the minimum wealth of the top 10 per cent. Missing years before 1923 were more difficult to estimate. The basic method adopted was to find series of data which bore a reasonably consistent relationship to that of total personal wealth over the period. Tests were made with several series such as national income and its components: national debt, money debt, and gross capital stock (and combinations thereof). The most promising proxy turned out to be that of gross capital stock obtained from Feinstein (1972) for which a fairly steady relationship to gross personal wealth was observed between 1923 and 1930.

Figures for total personal wealth before 1923 are therefore estimated in a somewhat cavalier fashion, which appeared nevertheless to be the best available. Fortunately, however, an independent test of the estimate for 1911–13 was possible. The estimates of Daniels and Campion (1936) afford the basis for this. Their mean estimate of total personal wealth in 1924–30 is approximately 10 per cent below that of Atkinson and Harrison. If one compares the estimates of total personal wealth of Daniels and Campion raised by 10 per cent with that of gross capital stock for the years 1911–13, the results are £7,158m. compared with £8,040m. It was felt that these were tolerably close given the alternatives possible and the uses made of the data.

For the years prior to 1923, therefore, gross capital stock was used to estimate total personal wealth for 1900–13 and 1919–22 (years for which these data were available). Missing data for years between 1914 and 1918 were obtained by graphical interpolation.

The entire series is a smoothed three-year moving average of the minimum wealth of the top 10 per cent over the whole period 1900–73. The RWI was then constructed from this data.

NOTES

1 Data were also computed on the assumption of a Pareto distribution with little material difference in the outcome of the analysis.
2 If the distribution of wealth is strictly log normal then estimates of σ from other percentiles would be identical.

Method for Obtaining Unbiased Estimates of the Regression Equation for the Backward Tracing Samples

The object of this appendix is to expand the method used to obtain an unbiased estimate of the regression equation for the backward tracing samples. The forward tracing samples presented no problem. However, the method of drawing samples of wealthy sons and then of tracing the wealth of their fathers is for the purposes of the analysis contained in Chapter 7, looking at things, as it were, through the wrong end of the telescope. It does not reveal the role of inheritance for a representative cross section, and it does not provide the requisite data, which is a representative sample of *fathers* and the wealth of their sons. This appendix sets out the method used to 'invert the telescope' and obtain an unbiased estimate of the required father–son relationship.

Figure D.1 *Diagram of the Relation Between Sons' Wealth and Fathers' Wealth (Logarithmic Scales are assumed)*

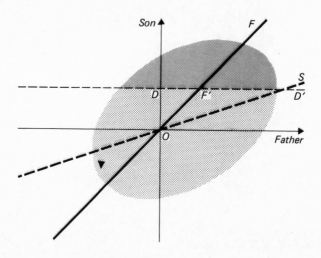

The problem may be set out with the help of the diagram. We suppose that in the whole population (if it could be fully observed) there is a scatter of points which may be put on to a graph showing the relation between the wealth of each son and the wealth of his father. In the usual way, two regression lines may be drawn – OS showing the relation between the average wealth of sons having fathers with a given wealth; and OF showing the relation of the average wealth of fathers to sons of given wealth. (These regressions are supposed to be linear, if the logarithm of wealth rather than absolute wealth is considered.) It is assumed, further, that the observed points in the sample lie in the upper region of the graph; they are shown as the heavier points above the dashed line DD'. A moment's reflection may convince the reader that an unbiased estimate of the portion of the line $F'F$ can be obtained (since it represents the means or horizontal arrays which are fully observed); but, from the data in the sample, there is no way of deriving the required slope OS (since the vertical arrays are truncated in the sample at their lower ends, and hence yield biased estimates). The problem is to estimate the slope OS from the observed slope $F'F$.

The problem can be solved if estimates of the variances in the whole population (not merely in the sample) of the wealth of fathers and of sons are available, as they are. From textbook formulae, one can then readily derive the following relation between the two regression slopes:

$$b_{sf} = b_{fs}\sigma_s^2/\sigma_f^2$$

Thus in the 1956–7 sample $b_{fs} = 0.605$, and from the published size distributions of all estates it is estimated that $\sigma_s = 2.18$ and $\sigma_f = 2.85$. From the above formula, we derive an estimate of the required slope as

$$b_{sf} = 0.35.$$

Evaluating the Importance of Inheritance – A Diagrammatic Approach

The following diagrams may help to make clear the different approaches that can be used in examining the importance of inheritance in transmitting inequality of wealth. We assume throughout that the logarithms of fathers' and sons' wealths are measured on the axes, as in Figure E.1.

This diagram sets out the position as we may suppose it to have been at the beginning of the century. The inequality in the wealth of fathers in the population was substantial, and can be represented by the distance *MK* (we can suppose for simplicity that this covers the full range of wealths and that the population is uniformly distributed within that range; at a later stage, if we wished to be more realistic, we can suppose that *MK* covers the central 99 per cent of wealths, which are log-normally distributed, and the span shown represents approximately three standard deviations on either side of the mean).

The inequality of wealth in the next generation ('the sons') is determined by:

(a) the degree of regression, which is shown in the diagram by a solid line *RR'* with a slope of 0·5 (this line shows the average wealth of sons, for a given wealth of their fathers; we assume that statistical problems of estimation have been solved as in Appendix D); and

(b) the amount of dispersion about that line, which depends upon the degree of enterprise shown by the sons, the riskiness of the environment etc. This is represented on the diagram by the dotted lines drawn parallel to the regression line; the wider the band between the dotted lines the greater is the element of enterprise and risk.

The combined effect of these two factors leads to the degree of inequality in the wealth of sons represented by the distance *AK*. This can be divided into two parts. The distance *R'S* is attributable to inheritance, and is equal to the product of the regression slope and the degree of inequality of the wealth of fathers. The remainder (*AK— R'S = AR' + SK*) is attributable to enterprise and risk, and is equal to the horizontal distance between the dotted lines.

By way of illustration, it is helpful to consider some extreme cases. If

Figure E.1   *Diagram showing the relationship between fathers' and sons' wealth at the beginning of the century*

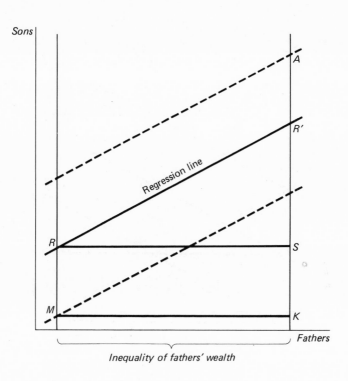

Inequality of fathers' wealth

there is no relation between sons' and fathers' wealth, the regression line is horizontal, and the distance $R'S$ reduces to zero; none of the inequality of sons' wealth is then attributed to inheritance. On the other hand, if there are no chance elements, the dotted lines merge, and all the inequality of sons' wealths is attributable to the inequality of fathers' wealths; this is true even if inequality had been much reduced, for example, due to progressive estate duty.

Let us next consider the observations on samples of fathers' and sons' wealth, as in the studies given in this book, and their graphical representation as in Figure E.2. We suppose that the sample is chosen such that the *sons'* wealths are greater than some truncation value T. All the observations thus lie in the hatched triangle ABC'. One possible measure of the contribution of inheritance is given by the proportion of sons that had 'rich' fathers, i.e. whose wealth exceeded a minimum value, H.

This is the kind of measure used in this study and it would be approximated by those observations in the trapezium $ACHG$, taken as a fraction of those in the triangle ABC.

Figure E.2 *Diagram showing the results of the father–son wealth relationship from data representing inheritance patterns at the beginning of the century*

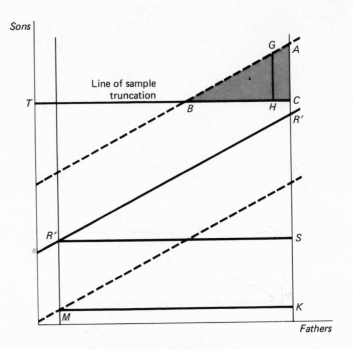

These measures seem attractive at first glance. Thus, if we consider a lower truncation line, the relevant triangles and trapezia all increase in size, and retain a technical similarity to their original shape. But a little reflection will show that their areas do not all change in the same proportion, and this leads to difficulties in finding an unequivocal measure of the importance of inheritance. This becomes clearer if we consider a gradual raising of the truncation level T. The triangle ABC grows ever smaller, and eventually becomes of zero area when $T = A$. However, the trapezium $ACHG$ (assuming H is fixed) becomes an ever greater part of the triangle ABC, so that on this measure inheritance is ever more important. These paradoxical lines of criticism must not of course be pushed too far; but they appear to cause some uncertainty on the results. In its simple form, as expressed above, the argument is based on a uniform distribution of observations; if we took a more realistic bell-shaped distribution, the results would not become quite so extreme, but one must expect a similar order of arbitrariness.

So far we have been concerned simply with describing our analytical tools. Let us now apply those tools to showing how contradictory results can be obtained using the two alternative measures. This may be done with the help of Figure E.3 where the same regression slope (of a half) remains as in the previous diagram, but there is a narrower band of dispersion about the regression line, reflecting the lower degree of risk etc. and there is a smaller inequality of fathers' wealths, as shown by a shorter distance *MK*. The inequality of sons' wealths is also reduced; but the share of that inequality attributable to inheritance has *increased*. *R'S* is now a *greater* proportion of *AK* than previously (in Figure E.2).

Figure E.3   *Diagram showing the results of the father–son wealth relationship from data representing inheritance patterns in the 1970s*

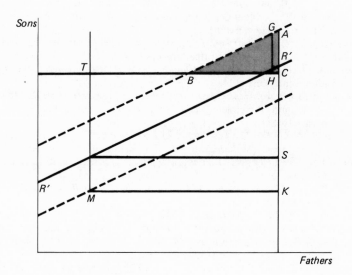

On the other hand, taking the measure of the type used in Chapter 3, the trapezium *ACHG* is now a smaller part of the triangle *ABC*, suggesting inheritance is of *reduced* importance. The precise results obtained on these approaches clearly depend on the values of *T* and *H*.

NOTE

1   There may in practice be a few points above *TBA* due to sampling error.

Select Bibliography

Aitchison, J. and Brown, J. A. C. (1957). *The Lognormal Distribution* (Cambridge: Cambridge University Press).

Alford, B. W. F. (1973), *W. D. and H. O. Wills and the Development of the U.K. Tobacco Industry, 1786–1965* (London: Methuen).

Astin, J. A. (1975), 'The distribution of wealth and the relevance of age', *Statistical News*, no. 28, February.

Atkinson, A. B. (1971), 'The distribution of wealth and the individual life cycle', *Oxford Economic Papers*, vol. 23, no. 2.

Atkinson, A. B. and Harrison, A. J. (1977), 'The distribution of personal wealth', in W. F. Maunder (ed.), *Sources and Nature of the Statistics of the U.K.* (London: Heinemann).

Atkinson, A. B. and Harrison, A. J. (1978), *Distribution of Personal Wealth in Britain* (Cambridge: Cambridge University Press).

Bateman, J. (1883), *The Great Landowners of Great Britain and Ireland* (London: Harrison).

Benjamin, B. (1968), *Health and Vital Statistics* (London: Allen & Unwin).

Board of Inland Revenue, *Inland Revenue Statistics*, published annually (London: HMSO).

Brittain, J. A. (1977), *The Inheritance of Economic Status*, Brooking Studies in Social Economics (Washington, DC: The Brookings Institution).

Central Statistical Office, *Annual Abstract of Statistics*, published annually (London: HMSO).

Cmd 2800 (1927), *Report of the Committee on National Debt and Taxation* (London: HMSO).

Colman, D. A. (1977), 'Assortative mating in Britain', in R. Chester and J. Peel (eds), *Equalities and Inequalities in Family Life* (London: Academic Press).

Daniels, G. W. and Campion, H. (1936), *The Distribution of National Capital* (Manchester: Manchester University Press).

Davies, J. B. and Shorrocks, A. F. (1978), 'Assessing the quantitative importance of inheritance in the distribution of wealth', *Oxford Economic Papers*, vol. 30.

Diamond (1975), *Royal Commission on the Distribution of Income and Wealth*, 1, Initial Report on the Standing Reference, Cmnd 6171 (London: HMSO).

Diamond (1976), *Royal Commission on the Distribution of Income and Wealth* 4, Report on the Standing Reference, Cmnd 6626 (London: HMSO).

Diamond (1977), *Royal Commission on the Distribution of Income and Wealth*, 5, Third Report on the Standing Reference, Cmnd 6999 (London: HMSO).

Feinstein, C. H. (1972), *National Income Expenditure and Output of the United Kingdom 1855–1965* (Cambridge: Cambridge University Press).

Galton, Sir F. (1892), *Hereditary Genius: An Enquiry into its Laws and Consequence*, 2nd edn (London: Watts).

Gray, P. G. (1958), 'Initial letters of surnames', *Applied Statistics*, vol. 7.

Harbury, C. D. (1962), 'Inheritance and the distribution of personal wealth in Britain', *Economic Journal*, vol. 72.

Harbury, C. D. and McMahon, P. C. (1973), 'Inheritance and the characteristics of top wealth leavers in Britain', *Economic Journal*, vol. 83.

Harbury, C. D. and Hitchens, D, M. W. N. (1976), 'The inheritances of top wealth leavers: some further evidence', *Economic Journal*, vol. 86.

Harbury, C. D. and Hitchens, D. M. W. N. (1977), 'Women, wealth and inheritance', *Economic Journal*, vol. 87.

Harbury, C. D., Hitchens, D. M. W. N. and McMahon, P. C. (1977), 'On the measurement of inherited wealth', *Review of Income and Wealth*.

Harrison, A. J. (1975), *The Distribution of Personal Wealth in Scotland* (Fraser of Allander Institute Research Monograph No. 1), University of Strathclyde.

Hirsch, F. (1977), *Social Limits to Growth* (London: Routledge & Kegan Paul).

Horsman, E. G. (1975), 'The avoidance of estate duty by gifts inter-vivos: some quantititative evidence', *Economic Journal*, vol. 85.

Horsman, E. G. (1978), 'The inheritance of wealth: the evidence of wills', *Oxford Economic Papers*, vol. 30.

Jeffreys, J. B. and Walters, D. (1956), 'National income and expenditure of the United Kingdom, 1870–1952', *International Association for Research in Income and Wealth, Series V* (London: Bowes & Bowes).

Lampman, R. J. (1962), *The Share of Top Wealth Holders in National Wealth, 1922–1956* (Princeton, NJ: Princeton University Press).

Little, I. M. D. and Fleming, J. S. (1974), *Why We Need A Wealth Tax* (London: Methuen).

London and Cambridge Economic Service (1970), *The British Economy: Key Statistics 1900–1970* (Times Newspapers Ltd for the London and Cambridge Economic Service).

Mallet, B. (1908), 'A method of estimating capital wealth from the estate duty statistics', *Journal of the Royal Statistical Society*, vol. 71.

Marriott, O. (1967), *The Property Boom* (London: Hamish Hamilton).

Meade, J. W. (1978), *The Structure and Reform of Direct Taxation*, Report of a Committee chaired by Professor J. E. Meade (London: Allen & Unwin for the Institute for Fiscal Studies).

Menchik, P. L. (1977), 'Intergenerational transmission of inequality: an empirical study of wealth mobility', mimeo., Institute for Research on Poverty, University of Wisconsin, Madison.

Merrett, A. J. and Sykes, A. (1966), 'Return on equities and fixed interest securities, 1919–1966', *District Bank Review*.

Neild, R. R. (1976), 'What is to be measured?', in *Royal Commission on the Distribution of Income and Wealth*, Selected Evidence Submitted to the Royal Commission for Report No. 1 (London: HMSO).

Peters, G. H. (1966), 'Recent trends in farm real estate values in England and Wales', *The Farm Economist*, vol. XI, no. 2.

Prais, S. J. (1976), *The Evolution of Giant Firms in Britain: a study of the growth of concentration in manufacturing industry in Britain, 1909–1970* (Cambridge: Cambridge University Press).

Rawls, J. (1972), *A Theory of Justice* (London: Oxford University Press).

Revell, J. R. S. (1965), 'Changes in the social distribution of property in Britain during the twentieth century', *Third International Conference of Economic History* (Munich).

Revell, J. R. S. (1967), *The Wealth of the Nation* (Cambridge: Cambridge University Press).

Rignano, E. and Stamp, J. C. (1926), *The Social Significance of Death Duties* (London: Douglas).

Rubinstein, W. D. (1971), 'Occupations among British millionaires, 1857–1969', *Review of Income and Wealth*.

Sandford, C. T., Willis, J. R. M. and Ironside, D. J. (1973), *An Accession Tax* (London: Heinemann Education Books for the Institute for Fiscal Studies, Publication No. 7).

Sandford, C. T., Willis, J. R. M. and Ironside, D. J. (1975), *An Annual Wealth*

Tax (London: Heinemann Educational Books for the Institute for Fiscal Studies).

Sandford, C. T. and Wright, P. M. (1969), 'Estate duty: inflation and long-term capital gains', *The Banker*.

Smith, J. D. (1974), 'Concentration of personal wealth in America', *Review of Income and Wealth*.

Spearman, D. (1975), 'In defence of wealth', *New Society*, pp. 450–2.

Ward, J. T. (1958), 'Farm sale prices over a hundred years', in the Centenary Supplement to *The Estates Gazette*, 3 May.

Wedgwood, J. (1929), *The Economics of Inheritance* (London: Routledge & Kegan Paul).

Whalley, J. (1974), 'Estate duty as a "voluntary" tax: evidence from stamp duty statistics', *Economic Journal*, vol. 84.

Index